HINTERLAND

Hinterland offers an answ
question 'what is creative
by showcasing the best ne
the fields of memoir, essay, travel and
food writing, reportage, psychoscape,
biography, flash non-fiction and more.

Our pages bring together work by
established, award-winning authors
alongside new writers, many of whom
we are thrilled to publish for the first time
and whose work, we promise, will merit
your full attention.

Often, the pieces you'll find in Hinterland
will straddle the boundaries between
strands and be difficult to classify:
we see this as a strength. Hinterland
intends to challenge, move, entertain
and, above all, be a fantastic read.

WELCOME TO ISSUE 5

Submissions
Hinterland is committed to paying writers and artists for all work we publish.
Please send us your work via Submittable:
hinterlandnonfiction.submittable.com
We accept submissions year-round and endeavour to reply within 4 months.
We regret we are unable to provide feedback.
There is a small fee of £3 per submission.

Subscriptions
An annual subscription to Hinterland
(four issues, print and digital) costs £34 U.K.,
£44 Europe, £54 Rest-of-world.
Digital subscription only, £20.
Please visit our website for full details.

Distribution
Hinterland is distributed worldwide by NBN International.
For all trade orders contact +44 (0) 1752 202301
orders@nbninternational.com

Advertising
Please see our website for current rates, or to discuss sponsorship please
contact us at hinterlandnonfiction@gmail.com

Acknowledgments
The Editors gratefully acknowledge financial contributions from the UEA
Publishing Project.

Find Hinterland online at
www.hinterlandnonfiction.com
or contact us: hinterlandnonfiction@gmail.com

ISBN: 978-1-911343-89-9
ISSN (Print): 2632-136X
ISSN (Online): 2632-1378

HINTERLAND®

THE BEST NEW CREATIVE NON-FICTION

Issue 5
2020

Issue 5

Editorial

'Hinterlands' is the theme for this issue and our writers have interpreted – as we hoped they would – that prompt as widely and richly as seems possible. Many pieces in this issue assume as their setting a land that is foreign to the author: Senegal, Haiti, the Lake District, Northern Italy, Central London and the Grand Canyon, but what underpins them all is their unflinching examination of the internal landscape - what Josephine Hart once referred to as 'the geography of the soul.'

With *Refugee Blues*, Ian Thomson allows us an exclusive peek into a new work, in which he unravels the legacy of his aunt's émigré past. Margaret Hedderman traces an expedition by the pioneering botanist Elzada Clover in a piece best described as a literary biopic. Lily Dunn, Hannah Storm, Ian Seed, Rob Atkinson and Jennifer Montgomery

Freya Dean is of Dutch-British descent. She graduated from UEA's Creative Writing MA where she received the Lorna Sage award and, the same year, was an Elizabeth Kostova Foundation Finalist. Recent work features in *The Real Story*, *Visual Verse* and UEA's Anthology series.

each revisit a pivotal moment in their past, in writing that has a quiet yet determined pull upon the reader, often to startling effect. There is also – thankfully – a sense of hope threaded through this issue, most notably in Laura Steiner's joyously cinematic *Friends For A Day*, Peter Pool's *Lessons From The Western Front* and Cecily Blench's *The Places We Return To*. Like every writer in this issue, Cecily is one to watch: her first novel recently won the Wilbur Smith Adventure Writing Prize and is contracted for publication in 2021.

We are especially excited to be publishing our first work in translation: Nina Polak's *No Petting* and, better still, to be including the original Dutch text alongside the English language translation, beautifully worked by Emma Rault. We hope to do more of this.

As always, happy reading.

Freya & Andrew

Andrew Kenrick has worked as an archaeologist and an archivist, a writer and an editor. He is currently studying for a PhD at the University of East Anglia, where he also teaches English Literature and Publishing.

Contributors

Rob Atkinson (*The Kingfisher*) is a zoologist by training, with a background in academia and the animal welfare charity sector. He was Head of Wildlife at the RSPCA and Chief Executive Officer of the Elephant Sanctuary in Tennessee, and now works as a consultant, focussing on creating an elephant sanctuary for Europe's captive elephants. In 2015 he gained an MA in Creative Non-fiction at UEA, achieving a Distinction and the Lorna Sage Prize for 'Work of outstanding merit'.

Cecily Blench (*The Places We Return To*) is a freelance writer and editor. Originally from Herefordshire, she studied English Literature at the University of York and worked for several years at an independent publisher in London. She has written for *Slightly Foxed*, *Reader's Digest* and *The London Magazine*, among others. She has a particular interest in travel writing, history, and intrepid women. Her first novel won the 2019 Wilbur Smith Adventure Writing Prize for unpublished manuscripts and is contracted for publication in 2021.

Lily Dunn (*Waiting For God*) is an author, mentor and lecturer. Her first novel was published by Portobello Books and her creative non-fiction has been published by *Granta* and *Aeon*, among others. She has edited *A Wild and Precious Life: Addiction, physical and mental illness and its aftermath*, a collection of stories and poetry from writers in recovery, to be published by Unbound in April 2021, and is currently writing a memoir about the legacy of her father's various addictions. She teaches creative writing at Bath Spa University, co-runs London Lit Lab and is studying for a doctorate at Birkbeck, University of London.

Margaret Hedderman (*The Domain of Courageous Men*) writes about the outdoors: environmental science, the use and abuse of wild places, and where we go from here. She is also the founder of the annual Women Outside Adventure Forum. Her experience as a backpacker, climber, and backcountry snowboarder informs and inspires her work. She is currently developing a collection of essays about self-propelled carbon neutral travel and climate change. Margaret holds an MA from the University of East Anglia and lives in Boulder, Colorado.

Tom Hutchings (*Summer Skies*) is our in-house graphic designer and photographer, based in the south of London. He's spent a lot of time this summer thinking about how people play games and how the interfaces of games (both physical and digital) can help or hinder their enjoyment. Have a look at his varied output at www.thorngraphicdesign.com.

Jennifer Y. Montgomery (*The Red Scarf*) is a writer, artist, storyteller, attorney, and pie baker who lives in Connecticut with her daughter. She grew up in rural North Dakota but has no discernible accent. She has also lived in California, Minnesota, Scotland, Israel, and Connecticut. All of these places have influenced her life and writing. Her poems have appeared in *Poetry Quarterly*, *Enclave*, *Jitter*, *Haiku Journal*, *Failed Haiku*, and elsewhere. She has told many stories on stage and has been featured on the Mouth storytelling podcast. She believes that truth is stranger than fiction and authenticity is the highest art form.

Nina Polak (*No Petting*) writes fiction, non-fiction and journalism. Her debut novel *We Zullen Niet Te Pletter Slaan*, was published in 2014, and her second *Gebrek Is Een Groot Word*, won the BNG Bank Literature Prize. She is an editor at *De Correspondent* and her most recent book is an anthology of essays on Dutch and Flemish Literature. *The Dandy* is a collection of five short stories translated into English and published within the *VERZET* series by Strangers Press in partnership with New Dutch Writing.

Peter Pool (*Lessons From The Western Front*) was born in Hull and now lives in Northumberland, after a career in mathematics education – a substantial part of which was spent in Third World countries. Current interests include writing and gardening, in both cases the attraction lies in the observation of the minutiae of day-to-day life.

Emma Rault (*No Petting in translation*) is a writer and translator from Dutch and German. Lit Hub voted her translation of Rudolph Herzog's *Ghosts of Berlin* one of the best books of 2019. She is a 2019 Idyllwild Arts Non-Fiction Fellow and the recipient of the 2017 GINT Translation Prize.

Ian Seed (*Partisans, I Remember*) teaches Creative Writing at the University of Chester, and has lectured in Italian language and literature. He is a poet, critic, fiction writer, editor and translator. He has published a number of collections of poetry and prose, including five full-length collections with Shearsman Books, the most recent of which, *New York Hotel* (2018), was selected by Mark Ford as a TLS Book of the Year.

Laura Steiner (*Friends For A Day*) is a writer, performer and improviser from Colombia. She started her writing career in New York where she graduated from NYU with a journalism degree and then moved to London in 2014 to pursue her interest in theatre. Theatre became physical performance which became comedy which led to improv. Whether it's writing words or on stage, narrative and story are at the forefront of her work. She currently lives back home in Bogotá where she spends most of her days perfecting her Spanglish.

Hannah Storm (*Aftershocks*) is an author, journalist and media consultant. Her award-winning flash fiction has been published online and in anthologies, and she has co-authored several non-fiction publications, including *No Woman's Land: On the Frontlines with Female Reporters* and the *Kidnapping of Journalists*. She is Director of the Ethical Journalism Network, and an acclaimed moderator and speaker on safety, mental health and gender in the media. She has recently completed a flash fiction collection, is finalising edits of a novel, and is writing a memoir. Hannah lives in the UK with her husband and two children.

Ian Thomson (*Refugee Blues*) is the author of an acclaimed biography of Primo Levi, a study of Dante and two prize-winning works of reportage: *Bonjour Blanc: A Journey Through Haiti* and *The Dead Yard: Tales of Modern Jamaica*. He also edited *Articles of Faith: The Collected Tablet Journalism of Graham Greene*. Ian is the recipient of the Royal Society of Literature's Ondaatje Prize and the W.H. Heinemann Award.

HINTERLAND

At Hinterland we are committed to publishing the best in creative non-fiction from around the globe.

We are always thrilled to feature work from established, well-known authors but have a particular interest in discovering new voices and in pieces that sit outside the usual categories: we ask only that it be a work of non-fiction.

We operate an open, year-round submissions policy and aim to read all work submitted within three months.

We pay for all the work that we publish and receive frequent interest from agents and publishers regarding our contributors.

Please send us your best work and we will endeavour to find a place for it.

Guidelines for submissions

- Submissions should be made via Submittable only. Please follow the link below:

- A small fee of £3 per submission applies to non-subscribers. Subscribers enjoy the benefit of submitting their work for free.

- All work should be new, previously unpublished material. If your work is subsequently accepted elsewhere, please kindly let us know.

- Pieces should not run to more than 5000 words. We accept anything from 500 words (very short pieces will be considered for our flash non-fiction slot). We also accept extracts from longer works, or works in progress.

- We warmly embrace writing on any topic, or from any genre, we ask only that it falls somewhere in the realm of non-fiction writing.

- Your work will be considered for all upcoming issues; it might help you to know that we operate a 3-4 month editorial lead time.

- We regret that, due to the number of submissions received, we cannot provide feedback.

hinterland.submittable.com/submit

Italian Partisans

Ian Seed

I

While I was waiting for the bus from Alba to the hillside town of Neive, a woman joined me and said, 'Buongiorno.'

She must have been in her mid-sixties. Her face was strong and beautiful, and there was something about her that seemed familiar. In fact, she looked like the widow of the author Beppe Fenoglio, on whom I was writing my PhD thesis, and whose birthplace and old haunts I'd come to visit. Perhaps it really was her.

Afraid to ask, I merely said, 'Neive is famous thanks to the stories of Beppe Fenoglio. No one else could write the way he did about battles between fascists and partisans in the rain on those hills.'

She smiled and replied in a strong local accent, 'Ah, so you foreigners know who Fenoglio is – you're more cultured than us locals.'

Only when I was on the bus to Neive, with the woman seated on the other side of the aisle, did I remember that Luciana had been dead for years.

II

On the last bus back, the woman was there again. She asked if I'd liked Neive, and if I found the hills beautiful.

'Very much so,' I said.

'It takes a stranger to see the beauty,' she said. 'People here don't see it.'

I was about to reply, when the bus turned a hairpin bend with a precipice just a few inches away. It made me think of Fenoglio's story about a truck full of partisans going over the edge.

'Don't worry,' the woman said, 'this driver does the route every day.'

By the time we reached the valley, it was growing dark and starting to rain.

'The hills are even more beautiful in the rain,' she said.

I nodded, then looked out of the window. What she said was true.

For the last part of the journey we were silent. I thought of introducing myself, but it didn't seem the right thing to do. H

The Kingfisher

Rob Atkinson

A stream has flowed beside my house for the fifty years I have lived here, and for four hundred years since the house was built. Before that, it cut its journey through a landscape that changed over millennia from oak woodland to fields and hedges. I wonder whether salmon or sea trout ever swam from the sea into the Severn, then the River Teme and into the Cradley Brook, before nosing into our little stream, water barely covering their backs. When we moved here there were a few brown trout in the deeper stretches, and every stone that my nine-year-old fingers lifted revealed a four-inch-long, mottled bullhead, with its flattened frog-like head and broad pectoral fins. Sometimes we'd see an eel as long as the brook was wide. Water voles grazed neat, circular lawns outside their burrows and once I sat and watched as, in a small pool below a riffle, black-and-white water shrews dived for shrimps and the stone-encrusted larvae of caddis flies.

Shooting blue along the stream were kingfishers. A kingfisher sighting was worth shouting to my mother in the kitchen, or my father in the garden. A second or less of zaffre electricity that flashed and disappeared into the tunnel of trees at the end of the garden, where the water was deep and shaded. Kingfishers were jewels, so much a part of the garden but rare and tropically beautiful. They were the brightest of our birds and the most ephemeral; jetting cobalt stars.

Once, through the kitchen window, I stood and watched as a star settled for a few seconds on a hazel branch into postcard prettiness. The kingfisher looked down into the stream beneath, its back half-turned to me, its head held at a slight angle. Small as a sapphire sparrow, with pale, pastel-blue rump and head, white chin and cheeks and a long, sharp bill. A glimpse of neat, rufous breast feathers. The kingfisher had an exquisiteness so perfect I could not absorb it before it dropped from the branch and darted away upstream.

Kingfishers are rare on this water now. American crayfish moved in fifteen years ago and drove out my beloved bullheads, eating the clusters of orange eggs they had laid on the ceilings of their homes under rocks. Trout don't live here anymore, either. The farmer upstream rejects pastoral for industrial agriculture, ignores the warnings of the Environment Agency, and goes on polluting the stream with silage effluent. I always wonder whether the last eel has gone, until, once every two years or so, I see one. Last summer it was hunting for crayfish, the grey of its smooth skin breaking the stream's surface in an arch, as it thrust its head between rocks. A few sticklebacks cling on, and I watch lonely, valiant males, with red underbellies and fluttering fins, defending their nests. Soon the crayfish will find these last few, and all the sticklebacks' harrying and hassling won't protect their eggs from armoured mandibles and claws.

Twenty years ago my family built a wooden fence at the back of the house to stop my father from falling in the brook. At that time, when he had yet to accept his frailty and his confinement to a wheelchair, my father would wander the garden unsteadily, ignoring warnings about the precipitous drop into the stream. We redesigned part of the house, so that my father could sit and look out through French doors that gave him a view twenty yards upstream, to the tree tunnel where holly and field maple joined over water that flowed deep in the narrow channel between their trunks. I sat with him one day, at the oak dining room table he had made years before, and looked out over the fence and the stream to the bramble-covered bank opposite. Beyond that was an old orchard with its battered remnants of apple and pear trees, which each year drop fewer fruit and more branches. The orchard trees are now too few to provide enough nesting hollows to sustain the little owls that once lived here, and which used to dip between fence posts, moving ahead of the car, when we drove down the track to the house.

My father found speaking difficult and we sat in easy silence. I wondered which nature was better: that of fifty years ago, with its little owls, trout, bullheads, water voles and water shrews, or of today, when birds once undreamed of fly above – ravens and kites and uncountable buzzards. Muntjac bark from the fields and – something beyond belief fifty years ago, when hunters with dogs and alien mink ruled the waterways – an otter now treks our stream. I remembered listening to it crunch crayfish when I stepped sleepless outside at 3am, calmed by its unseen proximity. Beside me my father dozed in his wheelchair and the memory of the sound of the otter's eating carried me towards dreaming.

My closing eyes opened at the sudden appearance of a bird on the middle rail of the fence. Its body was drawn out like a craftsman's awl: a tight, oval that constricted into a muscular neck, flared out to form a robust head, before tapering to a marlinspike bill. The bird must have shown other colours – a white bib beneath its chin, orange feet, cerulean along the forward edges of the wings – but I saw only a breast stained the colour of old blood. It stared straight at me along the sight lines of its bill.

The predator in the kingfisher was manifest in that under-view, and in what I could not see. Chest muscles that powered wings to fly through water, eight hundred times denser than air. Third eyelids protecting egg-shaped lenses that flicked from monocular to binocular vision underwater. The eyes lose acuity in the transition, but better judge the speed of fleeing sticklebacks, and the bird sharpens the image of its escaping prey through retinas designed to reduce glare.

With a catch held securely in its bill, the kingfisher will fly up, towards the other world it inhabits, breaking free of the viscosity of the stream, its lenses refocusing light from one part of the retina to another. Back on its perch, whip-cracking its neck, it will stun or kill the fish, and then swallow it headfirst.

The kingfisher's rust underside was that of the precise killer, who hunted an underwater world of currents and eddies, floating particles and viscidness. I beheld it momentarily, as the bird looked at me down its bill, its aquatic life dripping from its feathers. And then, fully in its other realm, the kingfisher launched itself into the air and, in an electric-blue flash, disappeared upstream. H

From the Greek ἔκφρασις (ékphrasis), meaning 'description';
a work of art produced as a rhetorical exercise,
in response to another work, real or imagined.

I Remember

by Ian Seed

(after Joe Brainard)

I remember my dad's 1930s black car with running
boards. He'd inherited the car from his father.
I remember it got stuck on a humpback bridge
with one of its wheels spinning over the edge.

I remember when I was four my mum sent me ahead
of her down the lane with a branch in my hand
to frighten away the hissing geese.

I remember jumping onto a donkey's back from a gate
and riding it bareback until it stopped at a hedge
and sent me flying into the next field.

I remember when I was six having a crush on a
blonde girl called Linda.

I remember learning how to tie my shoelaces.

I remember walking to school in the snow and not
wanting to arrive.

I remember a teacher in primary school used to
touch us up. I don't remember his name.

I remember when 'She Loves You, Yeah, Yeah,
Yeah' was number one.

I remember my mum and dad shouting in the night
and the woman downstairs banging on her ceiling.

I remember going to see *A Hard Day's Night* in a
Cardiff cinema. My favourite Beatle was Ringo.

I remember dancing on my own round the front room with the radio blasting out The Rolling Stones' new single 'Get Offa My Cloud'. My mum yelled at me from the kitchen to turn it down.

I remember doing bob-a-job for the Cubs in my green uniform, then spending the money on sweets.

I remember my mum's black eye and my uncle arriving in his van to take us to live with him and my aunt.

I remember Kaby, our Siamese cat, roaming my uncle and aunt's large garden, where we lived in a caravan. She'd been given as a kitten to my mum and dad on their wedding day.

I remember walking across Cardiff Bay to Barry Island with my dad. My mum told him to watch out for the tides.

I remember my dad barking back at an Alsatian dog behind a steel fence.

I remember travelling to Italy with him when I was eight. He was happier on his own.

I remember we stopped by the roadside in France on our way to Italy and a grasshopper hopped into my plastic mug of tea.

I remember the dark-haired woman with horn-rimmed glasses in Perugia. She was looking after me while my dad went to his conference. I remember the press of her thigh close to mine on a city bus.

I remember the last steam trains I saw, trainspotting with my dad.

I remember go-karting down a street and almost being run over by a bus because I didn't want to stop.

I remember stealing cigarettes and sweets from the newsagent's after my mum and dad got divorced.

I remember throwing stones from a bridge onto the motorway until a man told me to stop.

I remember the first time I saw a James Bond film with my dad. Was that before or after he'd split up with Mum?

I remember rolling newspaper twigs to light the fire and squabbling with my sister over who should sit closest to it.

I remember learning how to knot my tie.

I remember Diana Rigg in black leather as Emma Peel in *The Avengers* on a black-and-white TV.

I remember pop and crisps in the children's room at the Copt Oak Inn.

I remember the French teacher telling me off for picking my nose in class.

I remember forgetting to dry my back after a swimming lesson and the feel of my soaking shirt all afternoon in school.

I remember fish and chips scalding the roof of my mouth.

I remember running in the woods with Martin and his half-collie Jess.

I remember I was good at cross-country running, but I wanted to be good at football.

I remember I was with Martin in the woods and he said he'd teach me how to wank. He was a year older than me and knew everything.

I remember my grandma didn't like him because he had long hair.

I remember he got his girlfriend pregnant when they were both fifteen.

I remember I went to live with Martin's family on their farm when my sister died and my mum couldn't get out of bed.

I remember getting asthma from the hay.

I remember Martin took me on the back of his motorbike – a 500cc Triumph – telling me to lean with the bike when we went round a bend.

I remember being jealous of Martin's sideburns. I still hadn't started to shave.

I remember the boy with glasses who wanted to fight with me at school. I wouldn't fight someone in glasses, I told him, so he took them off and put them on the desk between us. I picked them up and put them on. You wouldn't fight someone wearing glasses, would you, I said.

I remember that the boy who wanted to start a fight later gave me an original 1962 Elvis single with 'Rock-a-Hula Baby' on one side, and 'Can't Help Falling in Love' on the other. It belonged to his older brother.

I remember the creepy bus conductor, who'd brush the back of his hand against a boy's arse when the bus was packed.

I remember reading *Catcher in the Rye* and wanting to drop out of school so that I could be like Holden.

I remember taking the night train on my own from Leicester to Aberdeen to see my dad. There were two men with me in the compartment who read out the dirty bits from a Micky Spillane book.

I remember the surrealism of Philip Lamantia in *Penguin Modern Poets 13*. It wasn't like anything we were studying at school.

I remember my grandpa, who'd been a stretcher-bearer in the First World War, came to live with us after my grandma died. My mum was remarried by then.

I remember my first proper kiss with a girl. I was on a youth-hostelling holiday with Nick in the Peak District. David Bowie's 'Rebel Rebel' was playing on the jukebox.

I remember going to Brees record shop in Leicester, and sitting in a sweaty booth where you could listen to one whole side of an album for free.

I remember going with Nick to see Dr. Feelgood at De Montfort Hall. We hitch-hiked around the country, following them on tour. They were better than The Rolling Stones.

I remember I kept failing Maths.

I remember getting drunk at the Copt Oak Inn and my stepfather shouting when I puked up at home.

I remember the sweeping rain on the first day of my A levels.

I remember working in a soap factory over the summer and being frisked on the way out because someone had been stealing soap.

I remember hitch-hiking to the Lake District on my own. I discovered Henry Miller's *Tropic of Capricorn* in Windermere library.

I remember losing my virginity to Anne, a law student. She knew more than I did.

I remember my mum waving goodbye. H

Refugee

Blues

by Ian Thomson

My aunt was a political refugee from East-Central Europe. Her life in postwar Britain was obscured for many years by secrets kept by her family: secrets and a sense of shame seemed to suffuse her life. She was an artist, but at some point she gave away most of her paintings. Nobody knows where they are now; perhaps they were destroyed. In the 1950s she had been a student at the Royal College of Art under Professor Carel Weight, the 'Alfred Hitchcock of British painting'. Her name was Maret Haugas.

On Maret's death in 2006 I gathered her letters, photographs, medical casefiles, and boxfuls of Royal College of Art ephemera (gallery catalogues, invitations to exhibitions). Much was missing from the jigsaw-puzzle of her past but it was clear to me that Maret had quite a life story. The mystery of who she was prompted me to search deeper into the material. I felt an aggrieved bewilderment and sadness as I did so. Every family has its own myth and ours was that pretty well everything associated with Maret was a source of shame. It was said that she had a demanding and difficult temperament; that she was not liked. Yet she had always been kind to me.

In 1960 my aunt was diagnosed with schizophrenia and sectioned in a psychiatric hospital outside Epsom in Surrey. Her career as an artist was over by the time I was born a year later, in 1961. Inevitably my childhood memory of her is patchy. Some quaint expressions ('What the Dickens!'), a taste of cigarette smoke from a kiss, the oddly accented English. In the 1960s when I knew her she was living with her parents in St Albans on the London commuter belt. During the school holidays I often stayed in that house while my parents were abroad on business of their own. Maret was my mother's younger sister; they did not appear to get on. Maret rarely emerged from her bedroom upstairs and she seemed to harbour some secret hurt. Sometimes she called me in for a talk. A smell of turpentine comes back to me. Stacked against the bedroom wall were a number of canvases – but when I asked my aunt about those she fell silent. I did not know it then, but beneath the façade of secrecy was an unspoken life of uprooting, displacement and mental illness – one, ultimately, of dashed hopes.

Carel Weight was the hand that buoyed her in her misery. In Maret I believe Weight saw a kindred personality: his own life was shrouded in enough sadness. As an official war artist in post-Fascist Italy he had painted fire-blackened buildings and street scenes of displaced humanity. In interviews he said he endured nightmares all his life. Weight was my godfather. My parents must have been introduced to him through Maret, who adored him. I remember a clownish-faced elderly man with an air of mild quizzical enquiry. For sixteen years Weight held one of the most important teaching jobs in Britain. In charge of Painting at the Royal College when David Hockney passed through, Weight taught the 'Pop People' (as he called them) Derek Boshier, Patrick Caulfield and R.B. Kitaj, as well as Bridget Riley, John Bellany and the singer-songwriter Ian Dury. Weight himself never received the critical recognition he deserved; he was overshadowed to a degree by the work of William de Kooning, Jackson Pollock and other American abstractionists. His day may come: David Bowie was an admirer, as was Kenneth Clark, former director of the National Gallery.

Maret had grown up in the 1930s with my mother Ingrid in the Estonian capital of Tallinn, a Tsarist-Germanic outpost with onion-domed Orthodox churches and cobbled medieval alleys. At the war's end the tiny Baltic republic was subsumed into the Soviet Union and dropped off the map of Europe. In the autumn of 1944, ahead of Stalin's advancing Red Army, the family fled on foot and on horseback until they reached safe haven in the British zone of Germany. In late 1945 Maret, barely ten, found herself in a Displaced Persons camp outside Bremen. She remained in the camp with her parents and sisters for three years until the summer of 1948, when she entered the UK via Harwich.

Her life was now hers to remake as she liked. In 1950, at the age of sixteen, she was enrolled for a six-year course at St Albans' School of Art. Among her contemporaries was Cyril Reason. Unassuming and reserved, Reason was a furniture maker's son from London, whose romantic style of image-making would come to the attention of the art historian Quentin Bell. Punningly known as C.Reason ('see reason'), Cyril was fond of my aunt and needed to be alone with her. She developed a breathless interest in him. Initially theirs was a platonic romance – what in those days was called an 'understanding'; it was the first of Maret's many unhappy relations with older men.

In 1956 she followed Reason to the Royal College of Art in London. Food rationing had just ended, Bill Haley's 'Rock Around the Clock' was high in the charts and duffel-coated theatre-goers queued to see *Look Back in Anger* at the Royal Court. The Painting School of the RCA was situated in a mid-nineteenth-century building behind the Victoria and Albert Museum on Exhibition Road. A grand flight of stairs led to the high-ceilinged studios and sculpture rooms where students painted on themes from the Bible and practised life drawing.

My aunt was no sooner at the Royal College than she found a new infatuation. Ian Mackenzie-Kerr edited the RCA magazine *Ark* and was a pupil of the illustrators Edward Ardizzone and Edward Bawden in the School of Graphic Design. He was four years older than Maret, and said to have the face of a medieval saint. Maret idealised Mackenzie-Kerr from afar. He later became a distinguished book illustrator and designer for Thames & Hudson.

It took less than a year for the relationship to go grievously wrong, with police involvement on charges of nuisance-making. One incident ended in Maret's arrest while she waited outside Mackenzie-Kerr's London flat. 'I don't think Maret actually stalked Ian, but still it was tragic', remembered Anne Martin, Maret's contemporary in the Painting School and a lifelong friend. While Mackenzie-Kerr said he wanted nothing more to do with my aunt, Maret sought only reassurances of his love. She was held in police custody and then admitted to a London hospital for 'disruptive behaviour'. Manic good moods had begun to alternate with black self-defeating thoughts.

What follows is an extract from a book I'm currently writing on the plight of the Baltic States in the Second World War and the refugee crisis it provoked; Maret's own story is woven into it. There is always a special risk when placing a family member into a work that incorporates a thread of 'self-biography' (as Samuel Taylor Coleridge called memoir). Not all those who recognise themselves within the story will appreciate their transformation. I acknowledge the betrayals – of privacy, respect and the familial ties that bind – that writing a book of this sort entails. Yet the discovery of my aunt's past was also in some measure the discovery of my own past: I persisted in my excavations.

Maret Haugas, St Albans' School of Art, c. 1951. Family collection.

Carel Weight, c.1958. Author collection.

In the summer of 1959, in spite of her illness, my aunt graduated with the RCA's equivalent of a first. At the convocation on 10 July the poet John Betjeman gave the address and afterwards congratulated Maret in person. The Painting School awarded her a Travelling Scholarship of £200 (£4,500 in today's terms), which promised hope and the possibility of future recognition. With it, Maret decided to go to Italy. 'I hope to paint in Florence and live as cheaply as I can', she wrote to Weight, adding: 'I should like to see Venice, Siena, Perugia and other cities and the surrounding country. I also want to see Rome.' Above all she wanted to research illustrations to the medieval Florentine poet Dante Alighieri, those by Botticelli especially, which she said she admired.

On 7 September 1959, having been issued with a pale blue United Nations refugee passport (sometimes known as a 'Geneva passport'), Maret was on the Dover ferry bound for France. At Paris she took the night train to Turin, and the next day, according to her visa stamps, she arrived in Florence. The effects of Italy's postwar 'economic miracle' must have been plain for her to see. Jazz rang out from the bars along the River Arno and there was a glint and a new flash about post-Fascist Tuscan life.

Thirteen years earlier, in 1945-1946, Carel Weight had painted scenes of Florentine bridges and buildings blown up by the retreating Germans. He had almost died when the second floor of a bomb-damaged palazzo collapsed under his feet. To Maret, though, it was as if the Tuscan capital had never known destruction. From her room in the British Institute on the banks of the Arno she set out to explore the birthplace of the Renaissance. At the Uffizi she queued to see Botticelli's *Primavera* (which had been stored for safekeeping during the German occupation in Osbert Sitwell's villa nearby). And on Weight's recommendation she visited the church where the Renaissance explorer Amerigo Vespucci lay buried, thinking how she would like to paint that.

After a week, according to psychiatric reports, Maret began to feel unwell. Delusionary and disordered thoughts and noises entered her head

After a week, according to psychiatric reports, Maret began to feel unwell. Delusionary and disordered thoughts and noises entered her head; she was sullen and hostile to British Institute staff and reportedly shouted from her bed at night. Asked to leave, she took herself to a pensione off Piazza della Signoria, where for days she remained confused and frightened. In the midst of this turmoil her friend Anne Martin turned up en route to Rome, as part of her own Travelling Scholarship. From Martin's recollection of what happened next, the events leading up to Maret's breakdown acquire a frightening reality. Martin was astonished to find

Maret 'impatient and snappish', and often lost in her own thoughts. She recalled that the owners of the pensione were 'very relieved to see her go'. When Martin spoke with Maret, very little seemed to register: her capacity to act rationally had gone or else was impaired. Yet somehow Martin was able to persuade Maret to accompany her to Pisa for the day. On the train Maret spoke in non-sequitur bursts about the awfulness of her life and how she wished to end it. Martin believed that the failed affair with Mackenzie-Kerr, if not the actual cause of her friend's emotional fragility, had played into it 'catastrophically'.

The descent into psychosis was at first sporadic, then precipitous: the last crushing episode before they sectioned her

On 12 October 1959, Maret returned to the UK. She looked ill and others who saw her that autumn confirm as much. The descent into psychosis was at first sporadic, then precipitous: the last crushing episode before they sectioned her. Christmas was spent with her parents in their St Albans house. The atmosphere must have been tense: it had been hard enough for her parents to assimilate as refugees into the UK; their daughter's illness put them doubly at risk of ostracism.

At some level my aunt's illness surely was a consequence of childhood trauma. Victor Gollancz in his bleak 1947 report *In Darkest Germany* speculated that children between the ages of twelve and eighteen who had been displaced by the Hitler-Stalin conflict would be left emotionally 'scarred for life'. In extreme cases some of them might transform into 'affectionless characters' doomed to lifetimes of compromised relationships. Gollancz's psychological insight was rare for the time. Few could guess at the disturbance – the neurotic aftermath – that lay ahead for these child survivors.

My aunt was committed to West Park hospital, Surrey, on New Year's Day 1960. Carel Weight did not know where his former student was, or what was being done to her. On 19 January he expressed his concern in a letter to Maret's father:

> I have been wondering how Maret is getting on. I have heard no word since before Christmas. I do hope she is making some progress. I wondered if there is anything I can do to help. Perhaps it might cheer her to know that the Scholarship money is awaiting her when she is able to make use of it. I would be pleased if you could manage to either drop me a note or 'phone me up.

Maret was under round-the-clock surveillance in West Park's acute-admission ward. Thin curtains separated her bed from those on either side in a ward that smelled of paraldehyde sedative. She was registered as patient 'No.9263', an 'Alien' of the 'Lutheran' religion. She had lost contact with reality and was hearing voices. Her mental state deteriorated as she tried to navigate her way in an altered, hostile world. She spent her 26th birthday – 10 February – on suicide watch.

After five months in West Park, on 2 June 1960 Maret was transferred to a psychiatric hospital closer to St Albans called Hill End, an Edwardian-era institution situated at the north end of Highfield Park. Her treatment there for schizophrenia involved sedation with liquid chloral nitrate ('liquid cosh'). Routinely the Control and Restraint team were seen to wrestle disruptive patients to the floor. Maret was subjected to electro-convulsive therapy, or ECT, followed at some stage by 'deep insulin' therapy, where a potentially life-threatening coma was induced after which she was resuscitated with glucose injected down a nasal tube. Seizures were supposed to occur during the therapy – the patient on the bed thrashing and spasming – and it is likely that Maret experienced these. The seizures were thought to be beneficial to the 'schizophrenic' mind. Anti-depressant medication in the form of Tofranil tricyclic –introduced for medical use in 1957 and sometimes used today to treat nocturnal enuresis – had so far failed to elicit any 'response'.

In the spring of 1961, as part of her hoped-for recovery, Maret was persuaded to return to Italy. She did so with her left-over Travelling Scholarship funds and with the support of Carel Weight. This time she stayed in a hilltop village outside Siena, Malafrasca, where Weight had put up the previous year with his artist friend Leonard Rosoman.
In a 1959 letter addressed to Royal College staff Weight had insisted that 'Miss Haugas be able to continue her studies out of England and be given as much help as possible'. After just one week she

was ill again. Re-admitted to Hill End, 'depressed and complaining of auditory hallucinations', Maret was ministered Mellaril, an anti-psychotic that suppressed anxiety but created a bovine-like blankness and sensation of dizziness. It was a pattern that was to repeat itself for the rest of her life: after the fiasco, the remission and then the relapse. Maret was in and out of Hill End for most of 1962, 1963 and 1964. Her ever more strange behaviours served only to isolate her from friends and family. About this time, according to Valerie Dolores Fabian, a contemporary at the Royal College, she joined the St Albans branch of the mystico-transcendental Subud cult, which encouraged uninhibited weeping and shouting combined with meditation. Like many Subudians (among them, Picasso's muse during the 1950s, Sylvette David), Maret came to feel that she was in contact with a divine reality and even at times taking divine dictation. Fabian was not alone in fearing that her dalliance with the cult might lead to harm.

She joined the St Albans branch of the ... Subud cult, which encouraged uninhibited weeping and shouting combined with meditation

'I bumped into your aunt in London in the mid-Sixties.' Fabian told me. 'Maret? I didn't recognise her. She seemed so transformed – edgy-looking, glancing over her shoulder.' By now there was no longer even a masquerade of normality; Maret was living in a world of her own and 'her face', Fabian recalled, had the 'pallor of a child – bleached out'.

Professor Weight, avuncular and solicitous to the last, did what he could to help. Over the next four decades he sent Maret over fifty letters and postcards; his support was one of the few good things that remained in my aunt's life. By his own admission, Weight worried 'rather a lot' about Maret; he routinely posted her money ('Please

'No sooner were the words 'Oh for my favourite eau de cologne!' out of my mouth than the postman arrived with a lovely bottle from you!'

accept the enclosed £5 note as a gift...') and made efforts to sell her 'discarded' paintings ('don't be surprised if you get a modest cheque'). He took her out to tea at the Victoria and Albert museum café ('I like a really good sergeant-major's brew') and to the Festival Hall for classical concerts. He bought her a new TV set and sent her colour photographs of his painting trips to Ireland, the Loire and Brazil made in the company of Edward Bawden and his wife Charlotte Epton. ('Ireland is a lovely lazy country with ever changing skies, rain, sunshine, pretty girls and good manners'). More: he kept Maret informed of the lives of her friends, among them her old boyfriend Cyril Reason, who between 1961 and 1962 had had three solo exhibitions at the Beaux Arts, then the leading London gallery for contemporary British painting. 'I cracked a bottle of wine with Cyril on Friday – didn't think he seemed very well – was having trouble with his teeth', Weight wrote to Maret in September 1969. Each Christmas, Maret sent Weight presents of bathroom soap and chocolates, as well as bottles of scent for his partner Helen Roeder. ('You must have a hot line through to the Virgin Mary!', Roeder wrote to thank Maret one Christmas. 'No sooner were the words 'Oh for my favourite eau de cologne!' out of my mouth than the postman arrived with a lovely bottle from you!')

Weight was now living with Roeder in a tall, four-storey Victorian house in Wandsworth, south-west London. The address at 33 Spencer Road served Maret as a haven between her hospital confinements. The overgrown back garden had a pond with koi carp and a stone sea-nymph fountain which Roeder liked to paint. Now in their late fifties, Roeder and Weight had come through interesting times together, having first met in the 1930s at Goldsmiths, where they became friends with William Burroughs' favourite English writer, Denton Welch (Roeder appears as 'Grace' in Welch's fiction, Weight as 'Randal'). During World War II Roeder had worked in London for the Artists' Refugee Committee, which unofficially involved the National Gallery director Kenneth Clark, with whom Roeder had a personal entanglement. It was Clark who sent Weight to Italy as a British government war artist in May 1945.

Roeder was a convert to Roman Catholicism whose sense of religious duty, undimmed over the years, encouraged her to practise good works. She worshipped at Westminster Cathedral and it was there that a priest introduced her to a former prostitute called Janey Winifred Hearne. Hearne had counted among her clients Graham Greene and the Conservative politician Rab Butler's younger brother Jock, with whom she is believed to have had a son. Having first come round for tea, Janey was soon made a permanent lodger at 33 Spencer Road: Roeder's charity, it seemed, stopped at nothing short of alms.

There is some suggestion that she and Janey were lovers. The Spencer Road house was 'dysfunctional and rackety', according to Roeder's godson Hugh Gilbert. Most weekends Weight went away in order to paint and to be with his woman friend of the moment. Neither he nor Roeder had children of their own ('We were too childish to have children', Weight observed). Visitors found Janey an unsettling presence and were at times even frightened of her. In a wire-mesh aviary on the ground floor she kept canaries, which she tended like St Francis his doves. Bird droppings strewed the floor. ('It was really quite disgusting', remembered Gilbert.) Janey doted on the house cats Biff, Ruffles, Jamie and Petal, but she had a violent streak and on one occasion threatened Weight in his own kitchen with a carving knife.

Not surprisingly Weight's 1961 *Portrait of Jane*, where Janey is seated in funereal black, engenders unease in the viewer; the fiercely concentrating gaze is emphasized by a mass of straggly dark hair and the sense of a world on edge. 'Janey was a very damaged soul – probably the most unhappy woman I've known', Gilbert said to me. She was fond of my aunt, though, and always enquired after her. In a letter

Portrait of Jane, Carel Weight, c. 1962.

Maret Haugas, St Albans,c. 1961.
Family collection.

Maret Haugas, *Nude Number One*, 1959,
Royal College of Art Collection.

Ruffles – in Carel Weight's bedroom.
Photograph sent to Maret Haugas, c. 1972.

to Maret, Weight wrote: 'Janey asks me to send her love to you and would tremendously like to see you'.

Each Christmas, Weight laid on a luncheon party for a select few artist friends, among them the Guyana-born Frank Bowling, the print-maker Constance 'Connie' Fenn and the Soho habitué Diane Hills, who was the so-called 'Kitchen Sink' painter John Bratby's long-suffering lover. Fenn and Hills shared with Maret a history of mental illness ('Connie has been, and still is, very round the bend', Weight commented of her to Maret in 1970). Maret laughed a good deal in their company. Amid the coloured Christmas lights the luncheons went on for hours, with Janey drinking quantities of cherry brandy. Maret too had begun to drink heavily; her father's home-made pear wine, stored in bottles in the St Albans garden shed, served as fuel for potentially self-destructive benders.

Her father's home-made pear wine, stored in bottles in the St Albans garden shed, served as fuel for potentially self-destructive benders

The gifted and undamaged art student that Maret had been before her illness took hold was only waiting to re-emerge, Weight believed; but it was not to be. The 1960s and 1970s were largely empty decades when Maret felt that her life had no clear purpose or meaning. In photographs from this time her eyes, anxious and wary, look as if they have seen most disappointments, and expect the rest shortly. Soon after her committal in 1963 she became acquainted with a young British poet,

David Chapman, who had been admitted to Hill End following heroin addiction. Chapman's account of his twelve-months incarceration, published in 1965 as *Withdrawal: The Evocation of a Confinement* (and set to free jazz the following year by the Spontaneous Music Ensemble), contains black-and-white photographs taken by Chapman with a smuggled-in camera. Patients are seen to cover sheets of paper with 'lecture notes'; others write verbatim reports of their 'inner voices'. One of the photographs shows a woman very like my aunt; she is walking across the hospital lawn, head bent low.

Hill End hospital had changed over the years; Chapman was to die of an overdose in his early thirties, but patients were no longer forced into cold baths, subdued into drugged submissiveness or electrocuted; they had been given a degree of autonomy. The 'therapeutic community' movement under the North American sociologist Ervin Goffman and the Scottish psychiatrist R.D. Laing had brought a spirit of forbearance and kindness to the UK asylum system. The watchword at Hill End was now cure rather than custody; this was thanks in part to Enoch Powell, who as Conservative Health Minister had condemned the asylum system in his famous 'water towers' speech of 1961 in which it was intimated that the Victorian-era lunatic asylums, 'brooded over by the gigantic water-tower and chimney combined', would save the government a good deal of money once they were closed; from their closure it would be a short step to their reform.

Royal College of Art

School of Painting Professor Carel Weight CBE RA HonARCA

Exhibition Road
London SW7

Telephone 01 584 5020

CW/mwpd

Miss Marat Haugas
4 Elm Drive
St. Albans Herts.

14th August 1970

Dear Marat,

You seem to have completely neglected your old friends. How about coming up one day?. I have been meaning to write to you to ask you for some time, but the fact that we have just put up one of your pictures in the Painting School office has brought the matter to a head!

I do hope that you are having a much better time now - please write soon.

Yours

Carel

(I love your painting – Mabs Dunlop. Painting School Secretary)

14. Oct 1982

Dear Maret

I felt sad that you are having such a rotten time. I do hope you will soon pull up. If there is anything I can do let me know. Would you like me to visit you? It would have to be sometime after Nov 8. as I am off to paint a portrait in Carlisle and then, on for a week to Southwold.

There are several interesting exhibitions in London including one at the R.A. called Pictures from Naples. – exciting Carravaggios and all very blood ~~thirsts~~ thirsty.

love from
Carel

P074 - MODIGLIANI A. (1884-1920)
Anna

Letter from Carel Weight to Maret Haugas, 14 October 1982.

Maret Haugas, 1959, Royal College of Art Collection.

Maret Haugas, c.1963. Family collection.

The connections that made up Maret's former life had not entirely disappeared. In 1967 *Queen* magazine devoted a June special issue to Royal College alumni and their work under Professor Weight; alongside colour plates of paintings by David Hockney, Kitaj, Peter Blake, Leon Kossoff and a Kokoschka-like canvas by Bratby, was a nude from the late 1950s by Maret Haugas. The nude was stored on site at the RCA along with my aunt's other abandoned art. 'You will be pleased to hear that we have your pictures hanging at the moment in the Painting School', Weight informed her.

London was officially swinging, yet the 'old' Maret was lost. Antipsychotic medication made her overweight; she felt ugly and misshapen and said she was ashamed to be seen in public. 'Don't worry about being plump', Weight typically reassured her, adding (on an undated postcard): 'I would like to see your new drawings very much.' Maret did not trust herself to present a coherent face to the world; but Weight, loyal as always, tried to coax her down to London. 'My magnolia tree is out in full blossom and should you care to come and do a painting of it, you would have to be fairly quick', he wrote to her on 3 April 1968. Maret did not take up the offer. 'You seem to have completely neglected your old friends', Weight scolded her good naturedly in a letter addressed erroneously but with strange pertinence to 'Marat': Maret's childhood home in Tallinn had been converted by the Soviets into a textile factory named 'Marat' after the French Revolutionary Jean-Paul Marat (who was done to death in his bathtub).

In a subsequent letter to Maret, dated 22 September 1971, Weight insisted that she 'come up to town', adding: 'If you feel nervous I would gladly meet you at the station and take you anywhere you like to go.' On his retirement in 1973 at the age of sixty-five Weight had established for the Royal College of Art a reputation that would be matched only by Goldsmiths in the 1990s. He painted prodigiously in retirement, transforming the streets of south-west London where he lived into faux-naïf landscapes of disquiet and Biblical apocalypse. While tidying his Putney studio one afternoon in 1981 he

[Weight] painted prodigiously in retirement, transforming the streets of south-west London ... into faux-naïf landscapes of disquiet and Biblical apocalypse

found a 20-year-old painting by Maret. 'I gave it a slight surface clean and then put some varnish on it and it now looks really splendid', he wrote to her. The painting ('It is rather large – I would think 48 x 36 inches') is now in the RCA's permanent collection where I went to see it. Swabs of dark-coloured paint combine with turpentine-thinned brush-strokes to create a shadowy atmosphere broken by mysterious areas of white light.

The work, untitled, is an abstracted representation of loss, perhaps, or of panic-fear. It dates from 1959, when Maret's painting *Dark Landscape* had been acquired by the Arts Council of Great Britain – an indication that even as anxieties accumulated darkly round her she was doing 'some of the best work in the country', according to Anne Martin.

Maret would never quite be free of physical pain. In 1974, aged 40, she contracted peritonitis, which was followed by a series of other, enervating medical upsets. 'I felt sad that you are having such a rotten time', Weight wrote to her in October 1982. 'I do hope that you will soon pull up. If there is anything I can do let me know. Would you like me to visit you?' He recommended an exhibition of Counter-Reformation Neapolitan art at the Royal Academy – 'exciting Caravaggios and all very blood-thirsty.' Maret appears not to have gone.

It must have been a constant stress for them to see their daughter lost in her madness

In the hot summer of 1986, alarmingly, she publicly removed her clothes and waded into the lake at Verulamium Park in St Albans. With no sense of illogic she explained to the police: 'My clothes were full of electricity', adding: 'There are millions of cars, all full of electricity.' Smelling of alcohol and dressed in a hospital property gown, she was interviewed at Hill End hospital by a consultant psychiatrist, who noted that she had been born in Tallinn in 1934:

> This is a 52 year old woman with a long history of admissions from the age of 26, initially diagnosed as schizophrenic, who usually shows labile emotions, childish behaviour and erotic elements in thinking.

In flat, affectless tones Maret spoke of her sexual feelings for a day-care patient she had met locally in St Albans. By plunging naked into the lake within view of the ancient Roman mosaic and hypocaust she had hoped to 'commune' with him (he was nowhere to be seen). Often in the past Maret had found herself attracted to hospital patients and staff members; among them, according to her medical notes, were 'three psychiatrists'. To this Hill End psychiatrist she made frequent references to her 'infantile moods' and hostile feelings. Mother, father and daughter were all three trapped inside the St Albans house. More than anger, however, Maret seemed to feel weariness at her situation – weariness perhaps of herself most of all.

She was prescribed injections of slow-release Haloperidol, an aggressive anti-psychotic which she had been taking, off and on, since 1960. For the record the psychiatrist noted: 'Childhood happy. No neurotic traits known.' For eight weeks at Hill End my aunt recuperated; by the time she was back home in October 1986 the threats she had made against her mother and father had been forgiven; they said they were willing to have her back 'permanently at home.' Her parents had been her primary carers ever since her first breakdown in Italy a quarter of a century earlier. It must have been a constant stress for them to see their daughter lost in her madness; they did not really know how to live with a life of such terrible unknowability and breakdown. H

DUTCH WRITERS' HOUSE
PULLEY FOR HOISTING STUFF
GRAPHIC NOVEL
FOR WORD-AND PICTURE-LOVERS
E-BOOK
VINCENT VAN GOGH
THE EAR INCIDENT IS SHOWN IN GRISLY DETAIL BY BARBARA STOK
andy
BY: TYPEX
A TRUE FAIRY TALE ABOUT ANDY WARHOL
CONTEMPORARY CHILDREN'S LITERATURE
LAMPIE THE LIGHTHOUSE-KEEPERS DAUGHTER CAN'T LIGHT THE LANTERN ON A STORMY NIGHT
TONKE DRAGT'S "THE LETTER FOR THE KING"
NOT THE DUTCH ONE
NOW ALSO A NETFLIX SERIES
IS NOT LIKE THE BOOK
TIURI IS ALMOST A KNIGHT
CHILDREN YOUTH
CLASSIC FICTION
"AN UNTOUCHED HOUSE" BY
IRAQI-DUTCH WRITER RODAAN AL GALIDI REALIZES IN HIS NOVEL "TWO BLANKETS, THREE SHEETS" THAT EXPECTATIONS CAN DESTROY AN ASYLUM SEEKER
HISTORIAN RUTGER BREGMAN WROTE "UTOPIA FOR REALISTS"
TRUE AI
POET MENNO WIGMAN 1966-2018 (TOO YOUNG TO DIE!!)
"BODY MY BODY HOW MANY HANDS OF HOW MANY STRANGERS REACHED FOR YOU?"
POETRY
TOMMY WIERINGA IS TALL, EVEN FOR A DUTCH PERSON
BOOK
THE BLESSED RITA
"EACH WORD RENEWS THE SILENCE THAT IT BREAKS"
FROM AWATER
GREAT PICK-UP LINE
MARTINUS NIJHOFF 1894-1953
FAMOUS POET (IN HOLLAND)
TAX THE RICH!
YOU ARE GOOD
IS ABOUT A MAN IN THE HINTERLAND OF HOLLAND FOR WHOM THE WORLD MOVES TOO FAST
THIS IS A PORTRAIT OF GOVERNOR: JAN SIX BY REMBRANDT (THE PAINTER)
ABOUT 23 MILLION PEOPLE SPEAK DUTCH (1.5 BILLION PEOPLE SPEAK ENGLISH)
THAT'S 20% OF THE WORLD
THIS BIRD SINGS IN DUTCH
"THE EVENINGS" A WINTER'S TALE BY GERARD REVE
PUBLISHED IN 1947 DESCRIBES THE ANXIETY OF BOREDOM AND THE HORROR OF LIVING WITH HIS PARENTS
AUTHOR HERMAN KOCH
HA
"THE DINNER" OFFERS FOOD FOR THOUGHT ABOUT BOURGEOIS LIFE
NL
NOVELIST, POET AND TRAVEL WRITER CEES NOOTEBOOM HAS FOR YEARS BEEN HOLLAND'S MOST LIKELY CANDIDATE FOR THE NOBEL PRIZE IN LITERATURE
HE'S ONE OF OUR MOST TRANSLATED AUTHORS
DESIDERIUS ERASMUS (1466-1536)
FUR COLLAR
HIDDEN DUTCH HISTORY!
SPEAK SLOWLY PLEASE
PHILOSOPHER AND ARTIST EVA MEIJER THINKS WE SHOULD RECOGNIZE THAT ANIMALS TALK TO US
YOUNG ADULT
THIS IS THE ENTRANCE TO "ESCAPE ROOM" A BOOK BY MAREN STOFFELS
HIS BOOK "IN PRAISE OF FOLLY" IS A BOLD SATIRE THAT POKES FUN AT THE FOOLISHNESS OF MANKIND!
PUBLISHED IN 1511
"WHAT IS LIFE BUT A PLAY IN WHICH EVERYONE ACTS A PART UNTIL THE CURTAIN COMES DOWN?"
THE DUTCH WE SPEAK AND WRITE TODAY TOOK SHAPE IN THE 16TH AND 17TH CENTURIES
ALFRED BIRNEY'S THE INTERPRETER FROM JAVA EXPOSES A CHAPTER IN DUTCH COLONIAL HISTORY

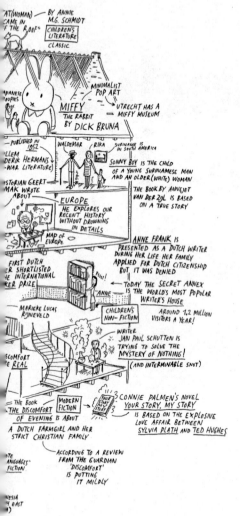

In Vertaling

Verboden te aaien

In Translation

No Petting

by Nina Polak

translated from the Dutch by Emma Rault

No Petting/[Verboden te aaien] is taken from *The Dandy* by Nina Polak, translated by Emma Rault, and is one of the chapbooks in the series *VERZET*, a collection that showcases the work of young writers working in the Netherlands. Published by Strangers Press in partnership with New Dutch Writing, the series launches across September/October and includes many award winners and nominees, including Karin Amatmoekrim, Jamal Ouarichi and Sanneke van Hassel.

New Dutch Writing is a campaign from the Dutch Foundation for Literature and Modern Culture to promote Dutch writing in translation in the UK. For more information please go to www.newdutchwriting.co.uk

In een poging om een verloren liefde te vergeten dwaal ik op een herfstdag door Artis. Niets beter om een gebroken hart te relativeren, denk ik, dan de onnozelheid van de lama, de verlichting van de luiaard, het opportunisme van de chimpansee. De dieren weten hoe je moet leven: compromisloos. Dat kun je van mij niet zeggen. Ik scharrel geagiteerd rond, probeer me te bevrijden uit mijn hoofd, waar haar stem nog klinkt, haar geur nog hangt.

Olifantenpoep, zeg ik tegen mezelf, dat is wat je nu ruikt, en niets anders. Ruik dan, kijk dan, recht voor je, de babygiraffe in de zon. Niet denken, kijken. De pelikanen, flapperend, alsof de revolutie is uitgebroken. Niet afdwalen, hier blijven. Daar, de pinguïns, waarvan ik ooit gelezen heb dat ze biseksueel en polyamoureus zijn.

Bij de roofdierengalerij moet ik zoeken naar de bewoners. Zitten ze binnen, de tijgers, de panters? Verstoppen ze zich? Achter de antieke tralies lijkt de begroeiing woester dan gewoonlijk. Rond de stalen bogen tieren klimplanten, de stenen ondergrond is mossig, er slingeren brokken beton. Het heeft iets post-apocalyptisch, deze sierlijke, negentiende-eeuwse kooi, overwoekerd door groen.

Dan zie ik het bord: ARTIS VERNIEUWT. De roofdierenverblijven zijn niet meer van deze tijd, staat er. De dierentuin neemt afscheid van zijn tijgers en panters. Hun betraliede huizen zullen worden gesloopt. Over mijn schouder lezen twee bezoekers

One day in autumn, I am roaming around Artis Zoo in Amsterdam in an attempt to forget a lost love. Nothing better to put a broken heart into perspective, I think to myself, than the cluelessness of the llama, the enlightenment of the sloth, the opportunism of the chimpanzee. Animals know how to live: without compromise. That's not something you can say about me. I scurry around anxiously, trying to break free from my head, which is still filled with her voice, her scent.

Elephant shit, I tell myself: that's what you're smelling right now. Smell it, and look there, in front of you, the baby giraffe in the sun. Don't think, look. The pelicans, flapping their wings as if revolution's just broken out. Focus–stay in the here and now. Look, the penguins – bisexual and polyamorous, I once read.

At the Predator Gallery, I find myself having to search for the residents. Are they inside, the tigers, the panthers? Are they hiding? Behind the antique bars, the vegetation seems wilder than usual. Vines are coiling around the steel arches; the walls are mossy; there are chunks of concrete lying around. There's something post-apocalyptic about it – this ornate, 19th-century cage, overgrown with greenery.

Then I see the sign: ARTIS IS MODERNISING. The predator enclosures have no place in this era, it says. The zoo is saying goodbye to its tigers and panthers. Their barred

mee, er wordt goedkeurend gebromd, geknikt.

'Het was ook zielig,' zegt de vrouw.

'Ja, dat was het,' antwoordt de man. 'Naar de apen dan maar?'

In het spookachtige hok projecteer ik de verdwenen panter, ijsberend van links naar rechts en terug, wantrouwig spiedend naar zijn toeschouwers.

Mijn lerares Duits reciteerde ooit een gedicht van Rilke, over een panter in zijn kooi. *Zijn blik is door het lopen langs de tralies/zo moe geworden dat hij niets meer ziet.* Ze had een rode neus, die lerares Duits, ze was een wilde, hield van lange nachten. Ik stelde me haar leven romantisch voor, met kunst, meer drank en nog meer vrijheid. *Als dans van kracht rondom het midden/waarin verdoofd een grote wilskracht school.* Ze pinkte bij het bevlogen voorlezen nog net geen traantje weg. De klas ademloos.

Wat trof ons aan die arme panter van Rilke? Dat hij wild was. Dat hij gevangen was. Dat hij wild en gevangen was. Wat moesten we daaruit opmaken? Dat je niet moet willen vangen wat wild is. Of, kinderen, bedoelde de dichter misschien dat we zelf allemaal eigenlijk de panter zijn? Wild maar gevangen, onderdrukt.

Het schijnt dat Rilke en Freud elkaar regelmatig ontmoet hebben. Ze voerden tot diep in de nacht gesprekken, wandelden door Duitse dierentuinen. Ze hadden het over van alles, maar toch vooral over de vergankelijkheid. Voor Freud was het antwoord daarop rouw – en dan niet die voorbarige rouw van jonge, melancholische dichters, maar gepaste rouw, op het moment dat die nodig was. Rilke was minder

homes are being demolished. Two other visitors are reading over my shoulder; they mumble and nod approvingly.

'It was a bit sad,' the woman says.

'It was,' the man replies. 'Want to go see the monkeys?'

I project the form of the missing panther into the ghostly enclosure, pacing from left to right and back again, eyeing his audience suspiciously.

I remember my German teacher reciting a poem by Rilke about a caged panther. *His gaze has from the passing of the bars/Grown so exhausted it holds nothing more.* She had a red nose, that German teacher, she was a wild one, liked late nights. I had a romantic notion of her life, full of art, more booze and even more freedom. *Like a dance of strength around a centre/In which a mighty will stands stunned, struck dumb.* She got so caught up reading the poem she was on the verge of tears. The class was breathless.

What was it that struck us about Rilke's poor panther? That he was wild, yes. That he was captive, yes. That he was wild and captive, yes-yes. But what conclusions should we draw from that? That you shouldn't try to capture things that are wild? Yes, or, class, was the poet trying to say that we are all of us that panther? Wild but captive–oppressed.

Apparently, Rilke and Freud met on a regular basis. They talked until late at night and took walks around German zoos. They discussed all sorts of things, but most of all transience. Freud's answer to that was grief–and not the premature grieving of young, melancholy poets; appropriate grief, when

zeker van zijn antwoord. Later bedacht hij dat het niet rouw was wat mensen nodig hadden, maar acceptatie. Het vermogen ons onder te dompelen in de wereld om ons heen, om zo, als gewonden, de moeder te worden van alle gewonde wezens.

'Zorg dat je nooit verliefd word op een gebonden man', lalde diezelfde lerares Duits op een schoolfeest in mijn oor (haar lippen waren zwart van de rode wijn, haar ogen stonden vermoeid). Ik heb haar ongepaste advies ter harte genomen: ik werd verliefd op een gebonden vrouw. Een tijgerin, die zich erop laat voorstaan dat ze wild is én geketend. Onuitstaanbaar. Onweerstaanbaar. Een natuurkracht. Vast ook ooit Rilke gelezen.

Ik zou me moeten onderdompelen in het dierenrijk om me heen, de Europese gieren zien in hun gigantische kooi, hun doodse pracht, hun roofzuchtige bekken. Maar ik denk weer aan de tijgerin, waar ze nu is, of ze zich wild voelt in haar kooi, of ze weet dat ze me verwond heeft.

De roofdierengalerij stamt nog uit de negentiende eeuw, zegt de directeur van de dierentuin in een persbericht over de sloop ervan. Katachtigen waren in die tijd een centraal aandachtspunt in de collectie. Ze werden gezien als de gevaarlijkste diersoort, de kroon van de schepping, en ze symboliseerden in de dierentuin het contrast tussen de wildernis en de beschaving.

Met het afscheid van het oudste en ooit het belangrijkste dierenverblijf zet Artis een stap uit de

grief was called for. Rilke was less certain of his answer. It occurred to him later that it wasn't grief that people needed, but acceptance. The ability to immerse ourselves in the world around us in order that we, the wounded, can become the mother of all wounded creatures.

'Never fall in love with a taken man,' that same German teacher slurred into my ear at a school dance (her lips black from the red wine, her eyes tired). I took her inappropriate advice to heart: I fell in love with a taken woman. A tigress, who prides herself on the fact that she is both wild and chained. Insufferable. Irresistible. A force of nature. Probably read Rilke too at some point. I should immerse myself in the animal kingdom around me, the European vultures in their massive cage–their gaunt beauty, their rapacious beaks. But once again I'm thinking about the tigress, wondering where she is now, whether she feels wild in her cage, whether she knows she wounded me.

The Predator Gallery dates back to the 19th century, the director of the zoo says in a press release about its demolition. Back then, felids were a key part of the collection. They were seen as the most dangerous species, the pinnacle of creation, and in the zoo they symbolised the contrast between wildness and civilisation.

By getting rid of its oldest and once its most important enclosure, Artis is leaving the 19th century behind and taking a step forward into the

negentiende eeuw, naar een heden waarin er een 'fragiele relatie bestaat tussen natuur en mens'. Door tralies kijken naar gefrustreerde, wilde katten is in de publieke opinie blijkbaar een archaïsch en barbaars verschijnsel geworden. Het dier tegelijk te kwetsbaar en te wild, de gevangenschap te expliciet, te zichtbaar. Over de jaren zijn de tralies dan ook al op veel andere plekken in het park vervangen door glas, zodat de moderne bezoeker zijn progressieve bezwaren even kan vergeten. In het apenhuis slingeren de doodshoofdaapjes (Saimiri Boliviensis) je tegenwoordig zelfs gewoon om de oren – geen zichtbare afscheiding tussen mens en natuur te bekennen.

Terwijl ik twee papegaaien gadesla die elkaar pikken met hun snavels (liefdevol of venijnig, ik weet het niet), bekruipt me een verbeten gedachte. Als we dan toch bezig zijn met het afschaffen van negentiende-eeuwse artefacten, wordt het dan niet ook eens tijd om afscheid te nemen van de meest barbaarse van al: het monogame, romantische huwelijk en al zijn verbasteringen? Het parlement der pinguïns zou het met me eens zijn. Kijk, hoe blij ze roetsjen op hun vette buiken, hoe ongecompliceerd ze waggelen. Niks geen jaloezie, bezitsdrang, daar is het toch veel te koud voor buiten. Alle pinguïns houden van alle pinguïns, toch?

De hyena's lachen me uit. Ze hebben door dat ik zoiets niet zo krampachtig zou denken als ook ik mijn tijgerin niet, om met Annie M.G Schmidt te spreken, het liefste in een doosje zou willen doen. *En je bewaren, heel goed bewaren/En telkens zou ik eventjes het deksel opendoen/En dan strijk ik je zo zachtjes langs je haren.*

present day, in which there is 'a fragile relationship between humankind and nature'. It seems public opinion has shifted and looking through bars at frustrated big cats is now perceived as archaic and barbaric. The animals are both too vulnerable and too wild–their captivity too explicit, too visible. Over the years, bars have been replaced by glass in many other parts of the zoo, allowing modern visitors to briefly put aside their progressive misgivings. In the Monkey House, the black-capped squirrel monkeys (Saimiri boliviensis) even come swinging right past your head, with no visible barrier between man and nature.

As I watch two parrots pecking at each other–affectionately or spitefully, I can't tell–a grim thought takes hold of me. If we're abolishing redundant 19th-century artefacts, why can't we also say goodbye to the institution of monogamous, romantic marriage and all its corrupted offshoots? The parliament of penguins would agree with me. Look at them happily sliding along on their fat bellies, waddling around without a care in the world. No jealousy, no possessiveness–it's much too cold outside for any of that. All penguins love all other penguins, right?

The hyenas laugh at me. They're onto me: they know I, too, would prefer to put my tigress in a little box, to use Annie M.G. Schmidt's metaphor. *And keep you there, I'd keep you there/And every now and then I would slowly lift the lid/And then run my fingers gently through your hair.*

In 1838 bracht Charles Darwin een bezoek aan de London Zoo. Hij was mijn leeftijd, 29. Zijn evolutietheorie was nog in ontwikkeling, maar die koude, vroege lentedag in de dierentuin betekende een doorbraak. Om zijn vermoeden te onderzoeken dat er een verbinding bestond tussen mensen en apen – toen nog een controversieel idee –, klom de wetenschapper in de kooi van de jonge, vrouwelijke orang-oetan Jenny. Van dichtbij keek hij hoe ze gereedschap gebruikte, observeerde hij haar flirtgedrag met mannetjes, speurde hij naar emoties in haar gezicht. In zijn notities lezen we bijvoorbeeld dat hij er zeker van was jaloezie waar te nemen bij Jenny als de andere apen meer aandacht kregen dan zij.

Maandenlang kwam Darwin terug om Jenny te observeren. Zijn ervaringen overtuigden hem ervan dat de verschillen tussen mensen en apen slechts gradueel waren: ze hadden gemeenschappelijke voorouders.

Het is een treffend symbool, man in kooi met aap. Darwin mag zijn bevindingen als zuiver empirisch hebben beschouwd; zijn omgang met Jenny weerspiegelt ook onze neiging tot antropomorfisme – het toeschrijven van menselijke eigenschappen aan dieren. In het huidige ethische debat over het voortbestaan van dierentuinen vormt die neiging een belangrijk argument vóór het houden en tentoonstellen van wilde dieren: wij, getemde stadsmensen, moeten ze van dichtbij kunnen bekijken om ons met ze te identificeren. Om ons te kunnen onderdompelen, te beseffen dat we een zijn met die jaloerse apen, die progressieve pinguïns. Dierentuinen laten dieren menselijker lijken en mensen dierlijker.

In 1838, Charles Darwin visited London Zoo. He was my age, 29. He was still working on his theory of evolution, but that cold, early spring day at the zoo marked a breakthrough. To investigate his suspicion that there was a link between humans and apes–still a controversial idea at the time–the scientist climbed into the cage of a young female orangutan named Jenny. He watched her from up close as she used tools, observed her flirting with males, searched her face for emotions. In his notes we read, for example, that he was sure he saw jealousy from her when the other apes received more attention than she did.

For months, Darwin kept going back to observe Jenny. His findings convinced him that the differences between people and apes were only a matter of degree: they had common ancestors.

It's a poignant symbol, man in cage with ape. Darwin may have considered his findings to be purely empirical, but his interaction with Jenny also reflects our tendency to anthropomorphise. In the current ethical debate about the continued existence of zoos, that tendency forms an important argument in favour: we tamed city people need to see wild animals up close in order to identify with them, to immerse ourselves, to realise we are one with these jealous apes, these progressive penguins. Zoos make animals seem more human and humans more animal.

Though Darwin identified with Jenny, it probably didn't extend to the uncomfortable realisation that keeping her locked up might be inhumane. Times were different back then. But the young scientist

Darwins identificatie met Jenny leidde vermoedelijk niet direct tot het onbehaaglijke gevoel dat het inhumaan was om haar op te sluiten. Het waren andere tijden.

Maar ideeën over vrijheid en gevangenschap had de jonge wetenschapper wel. In datzelfde jaar, nog steeds 29 jaar oud, weegt hij in zijn dagboeken de voor- en nadelen van het huwelijk tegen elkaar af. Niet trouwen betekent vrijheid, reizen (per luchtballon!), eindeloze interessante conversaties met vrienden. Trouwen betekent kinderen (‘*If it please God*’), constant gezelschap, een leven in Londen, de verplichting om iedere dag te wandelen met zijn vrouw. ‘*Could I live in London like a prison?*’ vraagt Darwin zich af.

Na een hoop wikken en wegen komt hij tot de wankele conclusie dat hij toch maar beter het zekere voor het onzekere kan nemen. Trouwen dus. ‘*Never mind, trust to chance*’, zo besluit hij zijn overpeinzing. ‘*There is many a happy slave.*’

We kunnen de dieren onmogelijk vragen of zij gelukkige slaven zijn. Mijn gekooide tijgerin gaat me het antwoord ook niet geven: ik heb haar vorige week uit mijn telefoon bevrijd. Het voelde goed, alsof ik me onzelfzuchtig inzette voor tijgeremancipatie.

Aan de andere kant van dit ontspiegelde glas zit trouwens de zilverrug, baas van de wereld. Hij kauwt op zijn wortel en kijkt met kalme verwondering naar de *Homo sapiens* voor hem. Arm wezen, zie je hem denken. Staat aan de enige goede kant van de kooi, erbuiten, en vraagt zich, naar binnen starend, slechts af waarom ze het liefste in een doosje gestopt wordt.

did have ideas about freedom and captivity. That same year, still 29 years old, he weighed the pros and cons of marriage in his journal. Not marrying meant freedom, travel (by hot air balloon!), endless interesting conversations with friends. Marriage meant children ('*if it please God*'), constant company, living in London, the obligation to go walking with his wife every day. '*Could I live in London like a prisoner?*' Darwin asked himself.

After much deliberation, he arrived at the shaky conclusion that it's better to be safe than sorry. To get married, in other words. '*Never mind, trust to chance,*' he concluded his ruminations. '*There is many a happy slave.*'

It's impossible to ask the animals whether they are happy slaves. My caged tigress won't give me an answer either: I liberated her number from my phone contacts last week. It felt good, as though I were fighting selflessly for tiger emancipation.

On the other side of this anti-reflective glass, by the way, is the silverback, ruler of the world. He's crunching a carrot, surveying *Homo sapiens* in front of him with a calm wonder. Poor creature, you can see him thinking. Standing there, on the only good side of the cage–outside, looking in–and all she can think about is why she's happiest being put inside a box. H

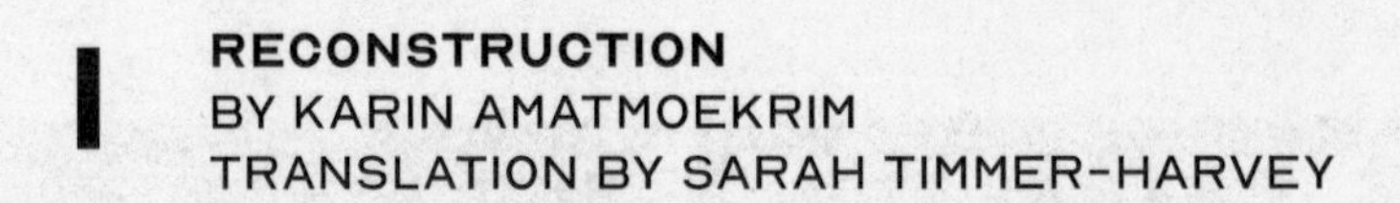

1 **RECONSTRUCTION**
BY KARIN AMATMOEKRIM
TRANSLATION BY SARAH TIMMER-HARVEY

2 **SHELTER**
BY SANNEKE VAN HASSEL
TRANSLATION BY DANNY GUINAN

3 **BERGJE**
BY BREGJE HOFSTEDE
TRANSLATION BY ALICE TETLEY-PAUL

4 **THE TOURIST BUTCHER**
BY JAMAL OUARIACHI
TRANSLATION BY SCOTT EMBLEN-JARRETT

5 **THE DANDY**
BY NINA POLAK
TRANSLATION BY EMMA RAULT

6 **RESIST! IN DEFENCE OF COMMUNISM**
BY GUSTAAF PEEK
TRANSLATION BY BRENDAN MONAGHAN

7 **THANK YOU FOR BEING WITH US**
BY THOMAS HEERMA VAN VOSS
TRANSLATION BY MOSHE GILULA

8 **SOMETHING HAS TO HAPPEN**
BY MAARTJE WORTEL
TRANSLATION BY JOZEF VAN DER VOORT

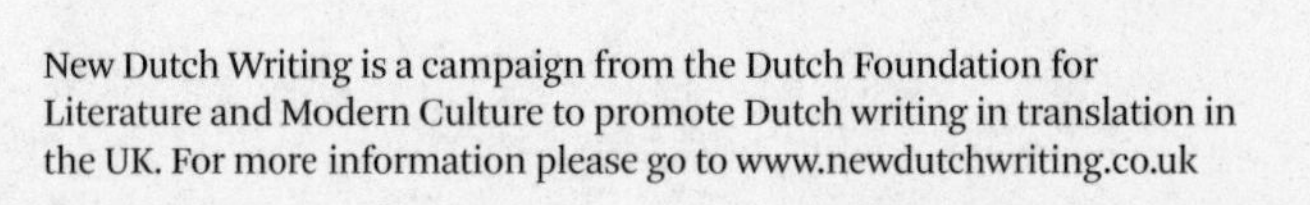

New Dutch Writing is a campaign from the Dutch Foundation for Literature and Modern Culture to promote Dutch writing in translation in the UK. For more information please go to www.newdutchwriting.co.uk

Waiting for

God

by Lily Dunn

We left our coats behind the bins so we could show the bouncers a bit of flesh. Shivered skin despite the shot of adrenalin. My whole body a blush when they finally ushered us in. We tripped down the mirrored stairs, a flash of red lipstick and teeth, our young cheeks a fire let loose in a blast of warm wind. Seventies funk powered up and pulled us under. All those beautiful people in the bar, fashionistas and wannabe models in purple, glitter and jump suits. We stood ablaze. Giggling and trembling. The Wag Club. 1989.

I met Charles on the dance floor. He wore a floral nylon shirt with big lapels, tight jodhpurs over shiny black boots, head wriggling with dreddy worms. He twisted his feet to Kool & the Gang, and laughed to himself, all shimmy and shine, when he saw me in concealer stick spots and a stretchy red dress.

'Yeehaa!' he shouted and narrowed his eyes, pouting to an invisible camera. He smelt of cocoa butter. In a haze of Blue Curacao and Bailey's Irish Crème, he told me he was a Vidal Sassoon hairdresser. He was 32. I told him I was 16.

He liked my hair, a lion's mane, long, blonde and unbrushed. He asked if I'd be his hair model.

I waited for him at the hairdressing salon. I waited on the padded, leatherette bench seats by the door and watched the ladies having their haircut. Sometimes I flicked through a magazine; sometimes I went to fill up my polystyrene cup from the water cooler; sometimes I picked at a small hole in the seat cover, slowly making it bigger. I waited in the basement. I stood at the bathroom mirror and tried on different coloured lipsticks. I sprayed hairspray and walked into its sticky mist. I hung about, always alert and ready. I waited among other young women waiting to do hair modelling. Sometimes we spoke, but often we didn't. One night I waited all night long, sleeping on the sofa while he fussed over models for a photo shoot.

Waiting. A promise that never comes. Time slows and morphs into a giant digit, bigger than you. It grips your ponytail, presses down on your head, leaves a pain at the back of your neck. The voice tells you to stay. It musses up your brain. Your mind won't settle; only the thought that he should be finished by now. He should be here. If you're not alert to it, he might not see you waiting and go off with one of those other models, the real ones, not pretend like you.

I was used to waiting. As a child, I often waited for my dad. Sitting on the wall of my school, hurling my feet in the air and scuffing up the heels of my Startrite shoes. Looking one way up the road, then the other, as the parents arrived in their comfortable cars and took their kids home. I'd squint at the shapes walking down the street, and searched for that height and bulk, a brown leather jacket and camera bag over his shoulder, that easy fluid walk.

I willed time to stop. To not pass, but the minutes kept banking up making a Jenga-like tower into the sky, each one loaded with his absence and my anxiety over why he wasn't there. Is he held up? Did something happen? Did he hurt himself? Did he go the wrong way? Did he get the wrong time? Did he get the wrong day? Did he forget me? Or was it me who got it wrong? Should I have gone to him? Did he disappear or die? My fear, those minutes, those wood blocks, tantalising in their instability.

My friends had boyfriends their own age. They sloped around the bedroom together, drank tea, and demolished a whole packet of Bourbons

I lost my virginity to Charles, uncomfortably in a white room, on a white bed, with a white lace bedspread. He told me it was his friend's flat. His friend's bed. That he slept in an upstairs room. 'She lets me sleep in her room when she's visiting her mum,' he said. He continued telling me this each time I visited, and slept in her bed, used her towels, took milk from her fridge. He never showed me his room upstairs, and I never asked to see it, because I believed him.

My friends had boyfriends their own age. They sloped around the bedroom together, drank tea, and demolished a whole packet of Bourbons. They revised together, and when their exams were over they drank too much and laughed their heads off.

They lived within the same block, a few streets away from each other. They were invited to the same parties. They fell in love. They fell out of love. They remained friends.

Charles lived on the other side of London. I'd walk to Highbury and Islington station and get on the train and pootle through North London – Camden where I'd normally get off for school, and on to Brondesbury, just at the back of Kilburn High Street. Sometimes we'd meet in town and I'd get the 38 bus and sit dreaming from the window. We'd go to the cinema in Leicester Square or go for a Chinese. In restaurants, I sat opposite him with my elbows on the table and watched him eat. I tested myself by seeing how many hours I could go without food before everything began to spin.

Sometimes I met him on South Molton Street at his salon and sat in a dark room, on a stage with other young girls with long hair. A tall camp man called Glen was rough when he backcombed. He was fierce with the pins and the donut, standing back to marvel at the huge hair cone that grew like a mountain from the top of my head. I smiled weakly with tears in my eyes while Japanese students came too close and clicked their cameras.

Charles didn't seem to notice that I spent so many hours waiting. He'd occasionally check up on me, 'Wassup?' and pout at his reflection. He'd spin his hairdressing scissors on his finger and say: 'You ready?' But he'd have to get his bag and coat and have a chat with his work colleagues about something really important.

I struggle with punctuality. My mother instilled it in me from a young age. She let me have a free rein on one condition: that I came home at precisely the time she asked me to. As a result, I struggle. I am always early. I wait. I was born to be a waiter.

My mother instilled [punctuality] in me from a young age. She let me have a free rein on one condition: that I came home at precisely the time she asked me to

After a year or two of waiting for Charles, I wondered whether the receptionist noticed, and what people imagined I was waiting for. My back ached, and my bum got sore on that bench seat. I dug my finger into the hole in the leatherette and pulled out a lump of stuffing. I rolled it into a ball and threw it into the bin. I watched the ladies with curlers in their hair, ugly in their shiny lipstick, their trivial noses in magazines.

Sometimes I couldn't be bothered to go to Charles's on the weekend. Instead, I'd go to Camden where a friend DJ-ed. I'd buy myself a beer and dance in the shadows. I didn't speak to anyone and ignored the mean girls who whispered and pointed at me. At the end of the night, I'd catch the bus home.

Years later, I walked past Charles's flat in Notting Hill. I was with a friend and we'd had a bit to drink. The lights were on and I said, 'Let's go call on him.' The flat was in the basement and we could see someone milling about in the living room, so we snuck into the front garden and hid behind a tree.

'Come on,' my friend said. 'We should go home.' But I wanted to surprise him. I crept down the stairs and knocked on the window. When he opened the door, I walked straight in as if it had not been years since we'd last met. 'Hello,' he said. 'Perhaps you could call next time.' I paced around the living room and snuck into the corridor like a territorial cat. I was tempted to extend my legs and wriggle my bottom, to project my spray all over the walls of his flat.

The lights were evening orange, and there was music behind a closed door. A warm smell of Body Shop lemon and grapefruit. He ushered me out of the corridor. 'She's in the bath,' he said. 'Maybe you should come back another time.' I knew it was his girlfriend. The one whose bed I had slept in for all those years, whose milk I had taken from the fridge. 'So you never told her,' I said, and tutted like he was a naughty boy. He shuffled, looked down at his feet, cleared his throat and directed us to the door. With a rush of alcohol in my blood I muttered, 'Bastard.' When we hit the street again we laughed like witches – 'did you see his face?' – and ran wildly with our arms in the air.

Jonno was six-foot seven, and a skinhead. He wore skinny Levi's over size-12 steel-capped boots. When we first met, he lived in a squat; a tall, thin Georgian house at the back of Camden Road with floor-to-ceiling windows and wrought iron railings. His living room was brown corduroy, with green velvet curtains closed to the traffic outside. On that first day, a group of us lost ourselves to mellow skunk and Dub with its reverb and echo. Minutes turned into hours, no one really speaking. When we got up to leave he told us a bunch of kids had broken in to the house the night before and had left a huge scythe in the toilet. He stopped at the bottom of the stairs to let me pass, and I felt dizzy when I looked up at him.

A week later he came to meet me at the Hungarian patisserie where I worked. When I saw him standing outside, I wiped the sugar from my hands and took off my pinny. In his van he asked if he could kiss me.

He got a studio flat in a Peabody block in Pimlico. From the kitchen window, beyond the red-brick flats opposite, you could see the corner of the Thames. The first time I visited, he made me supper and we lay together on the sofa listening to his records. When I said I had to go, he told me to wait until the song was over, but he'd turned the speed right down on the turntable, so it seemed to go on forever.

Jonno said he'd collect me in his yellow transit van. We'd go to the pub, or for a kebab. I'd be ready and waiting. I'd have chosen nice clothes especially: maybe a figure-hugging T-shirt or a new pair of jeans. I'd try to look casual on the doorstep or sit back on the wall and pretend to read a book. Eventually I'd stand in the middle of the road.

He worked in the music industry and went on tour. Sometimes I followed him. I followed him to music festivals and sat on the scaffolding as he did the light shows. I took drugs that he gave me and danced beside him as he worked. Sometimes the drugs took me places, other times I waited for them to come up and the more I waited the more I got stuck with myself. Like a kettle that never boils; like a phone that never rings. I followed him to gigs in Amsterdam and Köln. I sat in hotel rooms and watched the colour leech from his skin when he took another line of coke. I waited until the sun came up, and when I finally went to bed I waited to fall asleep.

Sometimes the drugs took me places, other times I waited for them to come up ... Like a kettle that never boils; like a phone that never rings

Other times, when he was away, I'd take the tube to Pimlico to water his skunk plants. He used special grow lights, which were on a timer, in a small cupboard. Jonno loved his plants. He spent many hours monitoring their growth, positioning them and the lights, and touching their sticky buds. He believed that if you loved them, they'd produce more THC, they'd give you something back. He spent time with his plants and sometimes I heard him muttering soothing words of encouragement, his large fingers teasing out their sweetness. I watered Jonno's plants, as he'd asked me to, and took off the buds that looked like they were ripe and ready. I carefully put them in a Tupperware box.

When he returned, I'd take food over, cook for him while he slept. I'd lay the table and wait for him to wake up. I'd sit on the sofa. I'd lie down beside him. I'd watch him. I prodded him. I quietly said: 'I'm here.'

He and his work partner moved into a new office in Islington. There was a ledge up high and Jonno lifted me and put me on it. My feet dangled, some seven feet above ground. He and his partner laughed and pretended to leave the room. They went through the door and closed it behind them. 'Bye,' they said and waved. 'See you later.'

I'd been waiting in the cold for nearly half an hour. I said: 'When you leave me waiting I'm stuck, like a balloon trapped in a tree'

Once I told my best friend I wasn't going to wait for her anymore. I'd been waiting in the cold for nearly half an hour. I said: 'When you leave me waiting I'm stuck, like a balloon trapped in a tree.' She laughed.

I tensed my fists and said: 'What if I need to go to the loo?'

'You go, dummy,' she said, like I was mad.

'What if you came while I was on the loo and you thought I'd left and you didn't stick around for me?'

She pulled a face. 'You waited for me,' she said. 'Why wouldn't I wait for you?'

I find myself in a new relationship. I want to arrive early for our date. I sit outside the pub one summer afternoon reading a book but keep glancing up at the cars as they pass, wondering which one will be his. He's held up at work. I feel my stomach knot and my shoulders tense. I want this relationship to be different. I don't want to be the girl, here, sitting pretty, waiting; her man trotting by and waving, glowing in the safety of knowing she will always be there, that she'll wait for anything.

When he finally arrives, he steps quickly from his car and takes me in his arms, eyes warm and bright. 'The meeting went on too long,' he says. 'I wish I'd left earlier.'

I smile and say I don't mind waiting. I keenly tell him I even quite like it. As I follow him to the restaurant, I curse myself as I have learned nothing.

Let's meet, we say: At six. Let's meet, we say: At 5.30pm. I'll take an earlier train; I'll leave that little bit sooner than I have to. Let's meet, we say, at 3.30pm. Under the clock in Waterloo Station.

But on the way, I take a wrong turn: I cross the bridge to the other side of the river, south instead of north. Weird, as I've walked this route plenty of times. I check my watch: ten minutes late – tick tick tick – fifteen minutes late. I panic. I rush.

Then I slow.

He's there when I walk through the concourse: a calm figure in amongst the shift and fury. His feet firm, his posture straight and assured, hands linked behind his back. He doesn't turn until I am right on top of him, my arms around his neck. We kiss beneath the clock. Holding onto me still, he leans back to look at me.

'You're here,' he says. The clock above his head tells me it's almost four.

'I'm late,' I say.

He looks surprised, then his face warms. 'I really enjoyed waiting for you.' H

The Domain Of Courageous Men

by Margaret Hedderman

It isn't whitewater. It's a frothing red wave, surging over boulders, crashing into itself, roaring downriver. Three handmade wooden boats - the *Wen*, the *Botany*, and the *Mexican Hat* - rollick toward it like flood debris. The *Wen* drops into the rapid first. It skirts around a wave where the current has formed a hole: the water running upstream and downstream at once. It could easily trap the boat and its passengers. Norm Nevills heaves at the oars, battling the river's will. He clears the rapids and shoots into a section of calmer water.

Norm and his crewmate, Elzada Clover, turn to watch the remaining boats. This is the largest rapid they've encountered, and the other boatmen are green and untested. Less than sixty people have survived the Colorado River and none of them were women. Elzada and her friend Lois Jotter hope to change that.

The *Botany* tears toward them. It rides straight into the worst of the rapids, oars swinging wildly. It flips into a trough and tumbles end-over-end, emerging upside down. Elzada scans the river helplessly for its two occupants. Then she spots them. One man clings to the capsized boat, while the other swims desperately for shore. Norm rows back into the current, chasing after the errant boat. They catch up to it and Elzada leans over the forward deck, grabbing the man's outstretched arm with one hand and the *Botany's* bow line with the other. Gene Atkinson scrambles aboard.

Norm and Gene pull at the oars, bringing the *Wen* within six feet of shore. They reach an eddy and for a brief moment they've escaped the mainstream. Norm takes the stern line and leaps for shore, but the river isn't done with them yet. The current rips the two boats back into the mainstream and Norm is jerked backwards into deeper water. The *Wen* and the *Botany* ride away as he swims to land.

Elzada and Gene careen into another set of rapids. Water rushes over them. They hold onto the bucking boat like it's a wild animal. Gene tries pulling them into another eddy, but the capsized boat is like a sea anchor, dragging them back towards the rapids. An oarlock bends under the strain. Gene shouts at Elzada to get the spare.

She grabs a knife and cuts the rope securing the extra oar.

'Hurry!'[1]

The knife slips from her hand and falls into the muddy water at the bottom of the cockpit. She fishes it out and cuts the remaining rope, freeing the oar. She secures the fresh oarlock, then suddenly realizes the boat is filling with water. Elzada bails frantically.

Gene spots another eddy up ahead. The river

---

1 Cook, p.46.

rages against his fatigued muscles, fighting to pull them downstream. At last, Gene guides the two boats toward the steep, rocky shore. There's no time to catch their breath. Elzada hands him the tow rope and says, 'For God's sake, hang onto it.'[2]

She takes the stern line and jumps. Knowing full well that Gene won't survive on his own if the boats are swept away, Elzada swims desperately to land. She scrambles up the rocks and ties the rope around a boulder.

Upstream at the Gypsum Canyon Rapid, Lois Jotter and her boatmate Don Harris row swiftly after the other man who is struggling to reach shore. They shoot the rapid, narrowly avoiding the hole, and pull him aboard the *Mexican Hat*. Bill Gibson is clean out of breath, choking on river water.

They head toward a sandy beach where Norm is waiting. He had sprinted after the *Wen* and the *Botany* for as long as he could, but eventually the boats were lost from sight. No one knows if Elzada and Gene have survived.

'The worry just about shot my nerves,' Norm wrote in his journal .

They pile into the *Mexican Hat* and chase after their missing companions. Norm takes the oars, his aching body fighting against the heaving water. Five miles and eight rapids later, the *Mexican Hat* floats around a bend in the river and they spot Elzada and Gene waving from shore.

---

2 Cook, p.47.

—

Like so many great adventures, the idea for the Nevills Expedition was sparked around a campfire. It was August 1937 and Dr Elzada Clover was wrapping up her summer vacation. She'd spent the last few weeks studying cacti on the Colorado Plateau and would soon return to the University of Michigan where she taught botany. She was a small, unassuming woman in her forties with short, dark hair and wire-framed glasses. At a time when women's fashion called for long, demure dresses and padded shoulders, Elzada often wore slacks and button-down shirts with the sleeves rolled up.

She was a small, unassuming woman in her forties with short, dark hair and wire-framed glasses.

Elzada had been staying at a lodge in the small desert town of Mexican Hat – an afterthought at the bottom of an empty map. It sits near the southern border of Utah, just a few miles from Arizona and the Navajo Reservation. If you wanted to get to Mexican Hat – and you'd really have to want to – it was a long, bumpy drive down a dirt road. Nearby, the San Juan River etched a winding course through the red-rock desert.

After dinner, Elzada and Norm Nevills – whose family owned the lodge – sat around a campfire, watching sparks disappear into the stars. Their conversation drifted into dreams. Elzada revealed that someday she'd like to take pack horses into the

Grand Canyon and conduct a full inventory of the plant life along the Colorado River. The interior of the Grand Canyon was still relatively unexplored and she imagined there must be countless new species. While there were some trail systems in place, Norm knew that hiking the length of the canyon would be near impossible. He offered a better idea: they could raft it.

Norm knew that hiking the length of the canyon would be near impossible. He offered a better idea: they could raft it

Just 29-years-old, Norm looked more like a man well into his forties; all those years working oil wells in the desert had taken a toll. He was tanned and lithe with a big, friendly smile that masked a shy and often self-doubting undercurrent. A few years before meeting Elzada, Norm had begun running rapids on the San Juan River and the upper Colorado. He was a natural entrepreneur and knew there was money to be had in the rafting business.

At the time, whitewater rafting could hardly be considered a sport. John Wesley Powell first journeyed into the depths of the Grand Canyon in 1869 and since then there had been only a handful of successful expeditions. There were no professional rafting companies, much less guidebooks. The first (and only) woman to attempt it had done so on her honeymoon in 1928. Both Bessie and her new husband Glen Hyde had disappeared at one of the last rapids in the canyon.

'I know we will be cut off from any hope of getting out in case of accident, illness or fright,'

Elzada wrote in her journal. 'Am really anticipating the thrill but know I'll be petrified.'

For the remainder of her stay, Elzada and Norm planned their expedition for the following summer. They would start at the town of Green River, Utah and raft 666 miles to the Boulder Dam[3] at Lake Mead, navigating Cataract and Glen Canyons before reaching the Grand Canyon in Arizona. Norm offered to build the boats that would run some of the most famous whitewater in the world.

When she returned to Michigan, Elzada was cautiously optimistic. At this early stage, the trip was nothing more than an idea, a gossamer dream that would vanish in the morning light. She mentioned her plans to few people, and those that she did, thought she'd lost her mind. After months anxiously waiting on word from Norm, Elzada finally received a letter in early January.

'Have been at work ever since you were here considering plans for the trip,' Norm wrote. 'You can definitely depend that we are going down in June.'[4]

Elzada immediately went to her supervisor, the Chairman of the Department of Botany, Harley Harris Bartlett. Although he thought it was a 'wild idea,' he couldn't deny it had merit. The University of Michigan was funding botanical research around the world, collecting specimens at an unprecedented rate for its botanical gardens. It seemed only natural that one of their botanists should be the first to survey the Grand Canyon.

---

3 Now known as the Hoover Dam.
4 Cook, p.11.

After receiving approval from Bartlett, Elzada got to work. In his letter, Norm had instructed her to find 'one more lady' and a 'college boy' for the expedition. She invited Eugene Atkinson, a 25-year-old graduate student who had grown up canoeing in Michigan. He was confident, if not arrogant. Elzada tended to see the best in people. Next, she asked Lois Jotter, her 24-year-old teaching assistant with whom she had lived the previous year. Lois was no stranger to the outdoors; she had once spent two weeks hiking in Yosemite while participating in a naturalist program.

When word got out that two women – scientists no less – were planning on rafting the Grand Canyon, it became national news. Articles often referred to them as 'schoolma'ams' and 'flora-minded', never hesitating to describe the heightened danger the river posed to their gender. Lois finally snapped at one reporter.

'Just because the only other woman who ever attempted the trip was drowned is no reason women have any more to fear than men.'[5]

—

The Great Depression was a decade of contradictions for women; the times demanded strong, unconventional female figures yet society pressed them into traditional molds. While aviators like Amelia Earhart and Beryl Markham became

5 Associated Press. Explorers Brave "Restless River". *Schenectady Gazette*, June 21, 1938.

household names, women were essentially banned from working as airline pilots. The airwaves were filled with radio melodramas about spunky, adventurous women, yet their audiences were typically at home doing the dishes. And while the First Lady Eleanor Roosevelt was once called 'the most liberated woman of the century' and her husband appointed more women to federal posts than any president before, the average woman was shunned from the workplace.

> **The Great Depression was a decade of contradictions for women; the times demanded strong, unconventional female figures yet society pressed them into traditional molds**

After the stock market crashed in 1929, fifteen million Americans lost their jobs. By 1933, the average family income had dropped 40%, and while most families could have used the additional money, no one liked the idea of a wife competing with her husband for work. A 1936 poll asked if women should work full-time if her family needed the money and only 35% said yes.[6]

Despite the adversity she'd already overcome to earn her PhD, Elzada's career prospects were limited. The daughter of poor Nebraska farmers, Elzada was the seventh of nine children. She was the first to be born in the family's wood frame house; the previous six children had been raised in a dugout shelter cut into a hillside. Farm life in the early twentieth century was unforgiving. It required every

---

6 Hargreaves, Mary. "Darkness Before the Dawn", p.181.

member of the family, regardless of age or gender, to pitch in. That work ethic, paired with her sense of adventure and ambition, had taken Elzada far.

Even so, the University of Michigan's Botany Department remained a boy's club and Elzada was its only woman. Although she had just been granted permission to risk her life for the benefit of the university, she was turned down for a full-time teaching position shortly before the trip.

Even so, the University of Michigan's Botany Department remained a boy's club and Elzada was its only woman

'Elzada isn't wanted because she is a woman,' wrote Bartlett. 'She has been unusually successful as a teacher of the younger students, and we need her precisely for that.'[7]

The prospect of an adventure in the American West, where man and woman faced the perils of nature as equals, must have seemed thoroughly liberating. And while the Colorado River would be her first time running rapids, Elzada Clover was certainly no stranger to navigating obstacles.

While Elzada organized logistics and supplies, Norm busied himself designing and building the three wooden boats that would carry them to Lake Mead. He recruited LaPhene 'Don' Harris, a 30-year-old engineer with the United States Geological Survey (USGS) to join the expedition and help construct

---

7 Clarke, Kim. "River Rat."

their boats. They had known each other for several years and had even run a section of San Juan River together in the years previous.

The flat-bottomed boats were sixteen feet long, five feet amidships, and four feet across at the stern. The bow and the stern were covered with a flat deck to provide two watertight compartments. Norm imported 2x2 oak for the framework and found a new type of plywood that was supposedly more durable and water resistant for the hull. They installed a single seat across the middle for the boatman to sit backwards. Unlike kayaks or canoes, which are paddled in a forward-facing direction, these boats would be rowed backwards through the rapids.

After an exhausting seven-day drive from Michigan, Elzada and her team rolled into 'The Nevills Place' just as Norm and Don finished painting the boats white. On the side of each, Norm had proudly scrawled NEVILLS EXPEDITION in big green letters. When they saw the boats, Gene and Lois pulled Elzada aside.

How come Norm got to name the expedition after himself? They were splitting the cost of the trip equally; didn't she think they should have a say in the matter? Not one to get caught up in such pettiness, Elzada thought nothing of it.

After a few final days of preparations – distributing gear, labeling food cans, and sorting rations – the group caravanned north to Green River where they met the final member of their party, Bill Gibson. The soft-spoken 24-year-old photographer from San Francisco had been recruited by Norm to document the expedition. It was an unusual assembly of characters, strangers for the most part, who would soon be spending over a month in very intimate quarters.

The boom and bust town of Green River sits roughly a mile west of the river's channel, surrounded by flat, white desert. The San Rafael Swell marks the horizon like a braid of broken ribs wavering like a mirage in the West.

On the morning of June 20th, the expedition signed autographs and waved goodbye to a small crowd of friends and family, as well as a few curious locals and journalists. An Associated Press reporter snapped pictures. His dispatch described 'the venturesome six' as they 'smiled happily and confidently as three frail … boats slipped out of this lonely southeastern Utah village.'[8]

From its headwaters in Wyoming's Wind River Range, the Green River cuts a vertical groove through the Colorado Plateau. It's a deep and powerful river, the primary tributary of the Colorado. Once it traverses the tortilla-flat basin where the Nevills Expedition put in, the Green becomes tangled in canyon country. It wends through a red maze, sandstone walls rearing up on either side. Alcoves eroded by seeping water are carved into the rock as if by chisel.

There was a strong headwind blowing up canyon on their first day. Each boat's crew took turns rowing

---

8 AP, pp. 6.

as the wooden oars blistered their hands. One particularly strong gust whipped into a dune at the top of a cliff and created a waterfall of sand. The meandering river was a perfect classroom for the

Everyone listened stoically to his advice; everyone except Gene who exclaimed, 'Lead me to the rapids!'

inexperienced boatmen and Norm was their professor. During the evenings, Norm discussed strategies for navigating tricky whitewater and taught them hand signals to use when they were beyond hearing range.

'I have done my best to impress the seriousness of this undertaking on them,' Norm wrote in his diary.

Everyone listened stoically to his advice; everyone except Gene who exclaimed, 'Lead me to the rapids!'[9]

Life on the river presented some unique difficulties for Elzada and Lois. While they were certainly challenging society's expectations, there were still some gender roles they couldn't break. The women would wake at least an hour before the others to make breakfast. At night, they were responsible for dinner. In between they darned the men's clothes, mended wounds, and provided the soft touches expected of their sex.

'Lois and I enjoy the way the men depend upon us for little things – just as men always depend on women to find this and that,' Elzada wrote. She started carrying matches in her pocket for Norm.

---

9 Elzada U. Clover Papers. 1938 – 1944. Bentley Historical Library, University of Michigan. 85109 Aa 2 UAl.

Norman Nevills and Elzada Clover on the muddy Green River.

The group on the river, from left to right, Del Reed, Elzada Clover, Lorin Bell, Lois Jotter and Norm Nevills before pushing off above 27 Mile (Tiger Wash) Rapid, Grand Canyon.

Elzada Clover, Norm Nevills, Lois Jotter, and Lorin Bell stand beside the *Wen* and the *Mexican Hat*, watching the rapids go by.

Members of the Nevills Expedition take a break at the Grand Canyon Overlook.
From left to right, Bill Gibson, Lois Jotter, Lorin Bell, Elzada Clover, Emery Kolb, and Norm Nevills.

'[He] gets all ready to smoke and never has a match.'

In the beginning, the women clumsily changed clothes beneath their blankets, but as the days wore on they simply asked the men to turn around. At one point on the expedition, Elzada powdered her nose for a photograph, implying women could still be feminine in the wild, or perhaps this was simply her way of poking fun at the notion.

As they floated down the winding river, Elzada sat on the stern writing in her journal. Whenever they hit a patch of rough water, her hand wobbled across the page. 'We are having a glorious time,' she scrawled. 'We have been getting along so well, all of us. We expect it to last.'

Cataract Canyon, "the Graveyard of the Colorado,"' lay just ahead. This was big water and ... the river was running at ... near 50,000 cubic feet per second

'Lady, get out your journal and give your last-minute impressions before seeing the Colorado. We are only three miles from it!' Norm told Elzada. The Green River dead-ends at a u-bend in the Colorado. At the intersection, a sandstone bluff looms overhead like a wild and lithic Flatiron Building. Heavy bands of red and grey rock stack one upon the other, rising to a sharp triangular promontory at the summit. At its base, the muddy red Colorado River washes over the olive-grey waters of the Green.

'There she is!' Norm shouted from the forward deck. 'She's a big 'un and she's a bad 'un!'[10]

The *Wen* led the way across the confluence. They navigated a small riffle and floated a further three miles. Cataract Canyon, 'the Graveyard of the Colorado,' lay just ahead. This was big water and in the summer of 1938 the river was running at peak flow near 50,000 cubic feet per second. Norm gave the signal and they pulled to shore just ahead of the aptly named Rapid 1.

Norm and the other men scouted the rapids ahead, while Elzada took the opportunity to collect plants. They had just made it to Rapid 2 when Bill saw a stray boat bouncing downriver with no one aboard.

'My God! There's the *Mexican Hat*!'[11]

Lois and Don's boat had untied itself and was getting away. Don dashed upstream as Norm shouted at him to get the *Wen*. He clambered across the rocky shoreline, quickly losing ground as the *Mexican Hat* sped away.

Elzada looked up in time to see Lois chasing after him. She watched helplessly as they leapt into the *Wen* and took off. Don spun the boat around and charged into Rapid 1, stern first. Lois waved goodbye as the *Wen* pitched and rolled over the crests of waves, plunging into deep troughs. Water poured into the boat. They ran one rapid after another before disappearing over a churning wall of water.

'Over me came the feeling that I surely must be tackling too big a job,' Norm wrote in his diary. 'Words can't tell the allgone feeling I experienced.'

---

10 Elzada U. Clover Papers. 1938 – 1944. Bentley Historical Library, University of Michigan. 85109 Aa 2 UAl
11 Webb, Roy, "High, Wide, and Handsome: River Journals of Norman D. Nevills", p.20.

He turned back and shuffled upstream in search of the others. In canyon country the sun sets early beneath the rim and dusk was coming on. Norm found the others sitting forlornly beside the *Botany*. What could have happened to the other boats? Were they pummeled against the rocks? Or sucked into a whirling hole? It was all too easy to imagine the worst. In a sober mood, they heated up a tin of food and passed it around. The spoons were in the missing boats, so they ate with sticks found along the shore. Something moved across the river and Gene thought it might be a deer. He reached for his rifle. In the growing dark it was hard to tell just what was moving across the river. There was a faint cry. A shout. Was that Don trudging up the opposite bank?

They jumped up and cried to their friend across the river. Don was alive! They quickly tossed everything back into the *Botany* and shoved off.

Don told them that Lois, as well as both boats, were in good shape. They'd found the *Mexican Hat* tucked into some rocks several miles downriver, completely unscathed. With plenty of food for the night, Lois had stayed behind to keep the boats secure.

'This river is really showing its teeth,' Elzada scribbled. 'We are right out here waging the biggest fight that one can ever wage and getting a big kick out of it.'

Full-grown trees ripped from their roots surged down the flooding river. Frothing at the crest, miles of furious rapids bellowed through the canyon. Elzada described the sound as an 'almost constant boom' like drums played by 'some savage tribe.' Norm cautiously let the team run what rapids he deemed safe, but ordered them to portage and line the bigger drops.

This was often more work than actually running the rapid. To portage, they pulled the boats – each weighing some 500 lb. – from the river and hauled them plus all their supplies down the shoreline. Small pink rattlesnakes shook their tails in warning. Loose rocks wobbled underfoot. The unfiltered desert sun fried their nerves. The work took a physical toll as well. Blistered feet. Bruised limbs. Bloody noses.

Miles of furious rapids bellowed through the canyon. Elzada described the sound as an 'almost constant boom' like drums played by 'some savage tribe'

Lining the rapids wasn't much better. After affixing ropes to the stern and bow, the boat was then guided through the whitewater from shore. While potentially less strenuous than portaging, lining ran the risk of flipping the boats or losing them altogether. It was a tedious journey through Cataract and Glen Canyon, as they made their way toward the Grand.

'Gene is inclined to be a little cynical of Norm's methods of handling lining,' Elzada wrote. 'It amuses me because he knows nothing about it himself.'

Norm was growing increasingly frustrated with Gene. 'He would soon wreck everybody if he were directing navigation.'

After the Gypsum Canyon Rapid where Elzada and Gene had been swept away, tensions began to run high.

Elzada and Norm floated ahead of the others, as Gene led a 'whispering campaign'[12] behind their backs. He griped about everything from the food to Norm's leadership, and soon the others were lured into the bickering.

'Gene is the vicious member trying to be an agitation and imagining he is so superior to Norm,' Elzada scribbled furiously. 'I feel very much humiliated since I am responsible for him.'

'Lois has been mighty rude and short with Elzada,' Norm added. 'Would like to drop her off at Lees Ferry.'

'It is really a wonderful trip and we are going to finish it if we are the only two left!'

The subject of changing the guard became more appealing by the day. Rafting the Colorado would be the greatest adventure of her life and Elzada was miserable at the prospect of her own students ruining it.

'Norm and I have spent lots of time trying to decide what is the best thing to do with members of the expedition,' she wrote. 'It is really a wonderful trip and we are going to finish it if we are the only two left!'

The Colorado River snakes around one final bend before emerging into a valley of parched benchlands. A gap in the barricade of imposing canyon walls, Lees Ferry provides the only road access to the river for hundreds of miles. It was an ideal spot for the Nevills Expedition to resupply and rest.

Their arrival on July 8th was several days behind schedule. Reporters had been anxiously waiting

12 Elzada U. Clover Papers. 1938 – 1944. Bentley Historical Library, University of Michigan. 85109 Aa 2 UAl

at the landing, writing stories about the group's likely demise. When the three boats pulled to shore, reporters swarmed around them, offering watermelon and inquiring about every detail of the trip. The Nevills Expedition made national news the following day.

To the outside world, the group appeared a team of smiling explorers celebrating a successful first leg of their journey, but a shakeup was on the way. Don left shortly after arriving at Lees Ferry, concerned that the expedition's slow pace would prevent him from starting a new job in early August. Norm happily replaced him with Lorin Bell, a wild young man fresh from an adventure in the South Pacific.

Then, Norm and Elzada decided to deal with Gene. They'd been off the river nearly a week and after several intense discussions and open arguments, Gene begrudgingly returned to Michigan. Immensely relieved, Elzada suspected he was secretly ready to go home. After a bit of scouting, Norm found Del Reed, a friend and local prospector to join them.

On July 13th, the team loaded their freshly painted boats under the skin-bubbling midday sun. Despite Norm's misgivings about her, Lois would stay with the expedition. They shoved off, waving goodbye to a small crowd before disappearing into the gates of the Grand Canyon.

They entered a landscape of immensity and contradiction: an infinite palette of pastel dreamscape and violent color; an impossible clash of land and sky; a bewildering blend of beauty and horror in the depths. The Colorado River plunges downward through time, gouging through sandstone, limestone, and shale. Flecks of juniper, sage and cacti paint the walls, diffusing a soft fragrance into the sparse, dry air.

'Lois and I were always glad when walls were sheer, insuring a ride through the rapids,' Elzada recalled.

For nearly 300 miles, the Nevills Expedition rafted past towering walls, winding through innumerable side canyons scoured by erosion and ancient lava flows. Bighorn sheep skipped nimbly along the steep walls above and the musical braying of wild burros echoed around them. Day by day, Norm led the newly emboldened team through a roaring cataclysm of whitewater; their hollers of fear and joy rolling over the waves.

'You've no idea how difficult it is to keep the mind on mere plants when the river is roaring and the boats are struggling to get through,' Elzada admitted.

As challenging as it was, Elzada and Lois had not forgotten their work. They stopped frequently throughout the day to collect specimens and often stayed up late pressing plants. When done correctly, plant pressing can preserve a specimen for hundreds of years. Elzada and Lois would wrap each individual plant, roots and all, in blotter paper, then lay them out inside a wooden press. Leather straps were used to squeeze the device shut, compressing and drying the plants for storage. While these numerous stops did slow the expedition down, Norm gradually grew interested in their work and even collected a cactus for his mother. Elzada and

Lois scrambled up cliffs, bushwhacked through side canyons, and sidled dangerously along the steep walls. Their work paid off with the discovery of four new species of cacti.

Any remaining tension or resentment was swept away by the power of the Grand Canyon and Lorin and Del brought fresh enthusiasm to the adventure. At night, they sat by the fire, singing, playing harmonica, and sipping whiskey. After a brief stop at Grand Canyon Village, the expedition added another member to its party: Emery Kolb, a legendary riverman who ran the Colorado River in 1911. He joined Elzada and Norm in the *Wen*, often standing on the stern as the boat rollicked through the rapids. As they neared the end of the canyon, Elzada grew melancholy with the prospect of leaving the river.

'These are wonderful days,' Elzada reminisced one evening. 'And if they should happen to be very brief I will have been more than repaid.'

On July 30th the Nevills Expedition approached the last line of rapids that lay between them and Lake Mead. Somewhere in this writhing surge of water Bessie Hyde had disappeared forever. Though by now they had run more challenging whitewater, the most dangerous incidents often occurred when a crew grew tired, or complacent, and let their guard down.

'Many times our boats rode safely through dangerous rapids to be almost wrecked by some freakish action of the water below,' Elzada wrote.

Norm looked over the rapids and believed his now-seasoned rivermen could manage it. One by one they shot through Diamond Creek Rapid, Killer

Fang Falls, and finally the last whitewater of the journey, Separation Rapid. After forty-one days on the river, Elzada and Lois became the first women to raft the Grand Canyon. Elzada looked back at the rapids with mixed feelings of accomplishment and guilt. It should have been Bessie.

After forty-one days on the river, Elzada and Lois became the first women to raft the Grand Canyon

Two days later the expedition was met at Boulder Dam by a crowd of reporters and autograph-hunters. This was a moment of many firsts: the first women to conquer the Colorado; the first commercial river trip through the Grand Canyon; and the first full botanical survey of the area. Elzada shipped the plant presses back to Michigan where her findings became the foundation of the desert collection at the university's botanical gardens. This work remains invaluable, as the only survey conducted before the construction of the Glen Canyon Dam, which destroyed many of the natural ecosystems along the river.

—

Elzada and Lois continued to work together for several years, publishing a paper in 1941 about their findings. After earning her PhD, Lois eventually moved to North Carolina with her husband and two children. She taught botany at the University of North Carolina until retiring in 1984.

The publicity the expedition garnered helped Norm launch a successful guiding business. He led six more trips through the Grand Canyon, as well as numerous others throughout the Southwest and up north, on the Snake River. To gain access to remote wilderness areas, Norm earned his pilot license and bought a single engine, Piper Super Cruiser. It was ironic, friends mused, that Norm was always so careful on the river, yet in the air was something of a daredevil.

Shortly after his final trip through the Grand in 1949, Norm and his wife Doris took off from a little airstrip near Mexican Hat. A few minutes into the flight the engine sputtered and died. Norm attempted an emergency landing on the highway, but the plane careened into a ditch and burst into flames. Both Norm and Doris were killed.

After the Grand Canyon, Elzada joined Lorin and Norm on another, briefer trip along the San Juan River before returning to Michigan. She continued to teach at the university and to conduct research throughout the Southwest and eventually in Latin America. In 1960, over twenty years after her historic trip through the Grand Canyon, Elzada was awarded a full professorship at the University of Michigan.

Although she gave numerous presentations about her adventure and never failed to mention it to her students, Elzada did not seem comfortable taking up the feminist torch. Her diary from the trip is professional, almost impersonal, as if she had known it would someday reside in the U-M archives. Did she share deeper thoughts elsewhere? Or was she simply adverse to conflict?

Perhaps her role as a feminist icon is an expectation we've placed on her retrospectively. Regardless, Elzada was better at letting her actions speak for her. Shortly before they left for their expedition, the *Detroit News* ran a story about Elzada and Lois. It described the Grand Canyon in stirring, emotive terms as 'the domain of only the most courageous of men.'[13] By the time the group returned, this line would have to be rewritten. ■

13 Cook, pp.18.

Bibliography

Associated Press. "Explorers Brave 'Restless River'." *Schenectady Gazette,* June 21, 1938. https://records.myheritagelibraryedition.com/research/record-10605-454244/schenectady-gazette
Elzada U. Clover Papers. 1938 – 1944. Bentley Historical Library, University of Michigan. 85109 Aa 2 UAl
Clover, Elzada. "Danger Can Be Fun." *Michigan Alumnus Quarterly Review*, Winter 1939, pp.103-113.
Hargreaves, Mary. "Darkness Before the Dawn: The Status of Working Women in the Depression Years", in *Clio was a Woman: Studies in the History of American Women*, eds. Deutrich and Purdy. Howard University Press, 1980.
Cook, William. *The Wen, the Botany, and the Mexican Hat: the Adventures of the First Women through Grand Canyon on the Nevills Expedition*. Callisto Books, 1987.
Clarke, Kim. "River Rat." University of Michigan Heritage, heritage.umich.edu/stories/river-rat/.
Webb, Roy, "High, Wide, and Handsome: River Journals of Norman D. Nevills" (2005). All USU Press Publications. 153. ps://digitalcommons.usu.edu/usupress_pubs/153
Collins, Gail. *Americas Women: 400 Years of Dolls, Drudges, Helpmates, and Heroines.* Harper Perennial, 2007.

Elzada Clover conducted the first full botanical survey of the Colorado River through the Grand Canyon. She and her assistant Lois Jotter were the first women to raft the Colorado.

Photo Credits

Image on p.91 is from the National Museum of Natural History, Smithsonian Institution.

Images on p.104-5 are from the Special Collections, J. Willard Marriott Library, University of Utah. Norman D. and Doris Nevills Photograph Collection.

Image on p.117 is from the Special Collections, J. Willard Marriott Library, University of Utah. Utah Photograph Collection.

The Places

M6

We Return To

by Cecily Blench

> Coming to it, we used to run down to the lake, dip our hands in and wish, as if we had just seen the new moon. Going away from it, we were half drowned in tears. While away from it, as children and as grown-ups, we dreamt about it. No matter where I was, wandering about the world, I used at night to look for the North Star and, in my mind's eye, could see the beloved skyline of great hills beneath it.

Arthur Ransome wrote these words in the introduction to *Winter Holiday*, the fourth book in his Swallows and Amazons series. He had intended the first novel to stand alone, but somehow found that he could not stop writing the stories that were based on his own childhood holidays in the Lake District.

The subsequent dozen books in the series move between Cumbria and Norfolk, and include overseas interludes, but in the end they always return to 'The Lake' – based on features of Windermere and Coniston – that forms the backdrop to the children's adventures. Ransome's love for and detailed knowledge of the area is evident in every chapter, and he imbues his young heroes with a fertile sense of imagination that turns the lake into an ocean, the end of the lake (when frozen) into the North Pole, a tributary stream into the Amazon River, and the highest hill into Kanchenjunga.

The places we know and love as children are imprinted on us, particularly summer holidays that are pictured in retrospect as idyllic and bathed in permanent sunlight. When I was a child my family would return to the same holiday places over and over. We lived in Herefordshire, in the far west of England, and because money was tight we almost always went on holiday to nearby Wales.

We had a number of regular haunts on the Welsh coast. For several years we went to stay with Isabel, a friend of my parents', who lived on a wild and craggy stretch of the Pembrokeshire Coast Path.

The thing I remember most vividly from those journeys to Cardigan Bay was the drive, starting very early in the morning, which took us over the rocky Preseli Mountains, our small battered car juddering up the steep inclines. We regularly had to stop to let the engine cool down, and often took this opportunity to swim in a mountain stream. The water was gaspingly cold, but there was an exquisite pleasure in sinking into the clear icy torrent, the rocks rough under our bare feet, while we looked up at the ragged hillside and the blue sky.

Like Ransome and his siblings, we had rituals for the journey that were completed without fail every year. Half-buried under sleeping bags and food hampers, books and beach towels, my sister and I competed to see who could be first to spot the sea, glinting on the horizon, with the obligatory shout: 'I can SEE the SEA!' Nothing I have done as an adult compares with the excitement of glimpsing the sea for the first time in a year, after interminable months at school. Time passes so slowly when you are a child, and what are now small pleasures were then tremendous events.

Isabel's house was in walking distance of a rocky cave formation known as the Witches' Cauldron, where in rough weather the sea churned in a furious frenzy, tossing spray high onto the cliffs above. In good weather my sister and I would run down the path that took us to sea level, and leap into the calm green water that lapped over smooth rocks. It was cold, as British sea swimming almost always is, but in my memory it was a tropical paradise.

When we weren't swimming we lazed in the garden, counted the hundreds of slugs that appeared on wet days, and painted pictures. Isabel was an artist, and she lent us watercolours, gave constructive criticism of our work, and treated us as fellow artists, which we loved. Helping my parents to move house recently, I found a painting that my sister had done of an ancient gargoyle that inhabited a lane near Isabel's house, his sneering stone face carved over a freshwater spring. She painted it around twenty-five years ago, but it had barely faded.

Isabel was kind but unused to having children around, and her health was poor. She liked to have us there, but the reality of having two lively children in the house did not suit her at all, and she was often tense and irritable. She lived alone the rest of the year, and I suspect she found our family's noisy ebullience very trying.

At some point she disappeared from our lives, in the way that people do when you're a child, and we stopped taking our summer holidays with her. I heard later that she'd moved abroad. I don't believe I ever saw her again.

It was cold, as British sea swimming almost always is, but in my memory it was a tropical paradise

Then there were trips to the Gower Peninsula, in the south of Wales, where we spent our holidays in a big leaky tent. These were our poorest years, I suppose, for the tent was old and tattered, and for supper we had pasta or soup or something else that could easily be cooked on an elderly gas stove. On wet days we played Scrabble and drank cocoa out of tin mugs. But the landscape in that part of the world more than made up for the simplicity of our lodgings, and we were never bored.

From our campsite at Llanmadoc you could run down towards the sea, passing through a little gate and a small stand of trees and then emerging behind the huge sand dunes that lie all along that coast. As soon as we started climbing the dunes we would take our shoes off, feeling the warm sand crunching between our toes. We'd hear the low roar of the waves, and at last emerge on the top and see the wide beach before us and, far away, the sea.

It's bleak and beautiful, Whiteford Sands, a massive stretch of beach that goes on for miles. I can still picture the pale sand, the rockpools where I fished for crabs, the rocky outcrops where we sheltered while eating our sandwiches, and the broad salt marshes further along the coast, exotic and faintly sinister. In my imagination the salt marshes were a lawless place, where pirates hid from justice and buried their treasure, and where you might be attacked by wild animals or be sucked down into the bottomless marsh.

In my imagination the salt marshes were a lawless place, where pirates hid from justice and buried their treasure

Every day we would walk along the beach for half a mile or so and find a place to settle, ideally with a cliff behind so that my parents could lean comfortably against it while they read their books and newspapers. Those cliffs were riddled with caves and holes. If we climbed high enough my sister and I started to see signs on the rock face that said things like, 'Caution: Unexploded Bombs.' During the war the area was used as a practice range by the army for firing heavy weapons, and many of the leftovers were never found. It gave the whole place a rather exciting feeling, knowing that we could be blown sky-high at any minute. I'm not sure if my parents knew how high we climbed; they were, on the whole, relaxed about potential peril, a rare quality for which I am still grateful.

Three or four miles along the beach was an abandoned lighthouse, which at low tide we would walk out to, picking our way through the thick mussels that encrusted the rocks around its base. My sister once told me that it was haunted by a dead lighthouse keeper who'd been lost in a winter storm, and for ever after I was very careful not to look too hard up at the windows, for fear of what might be looking back.

When I was twelve my parents scraped together enough money for a holiday abroad, renting a house from another friend, this time in the hills of Crete. From the airport we took a series of ramshackle buses that rattled around hair-raising gorges, looking in turn at the extraordinary views and the numerous ornate memorials to victims of road accidents.

I sometimes wonder what families who don't read do on holiday. For us it took up a good few hours of each day; in Crete we read throughout the hot morning, had lunch, read some more and then, in the softer heat of the afternoon, we ambled down through acres of olive groves to the sea, four miles away, stopping in the shade every so often to drink tepid water and gasp at one another. The rest of the day was spent on the beach, swimming, sunbathing, and, of course, more reading. When the light began to fade we straggled back up the hill, the air filled with the warm scent of olives and figs.

Near the end of our holiday, as we sat having supper on the veranda one evening, the bells of the nearby church began to ring, and soon all of the churches in the local villages were clanging frantically. At first we supposed that it was a festival of some sort, but someone shouted in English that there was a fire, and all at once we noticed the ominous flickering light, and peered around the back of the house to see that the mountainside above us was ablaze.

I remember my father packing clothes into a rucksack, as he and my mother anxiously discussed whether we ought to make a run for it. In the distance we saw trucks filled with men juddering up the hill, until they leapt out to beat at the fire with brooms, silhouetted against the flames, their efforts pathetically inadequate. Apparently a helicopter came in the end, and the next day the hillside was blackened. All I remember are the bells, and the brooms, and the primeval fear I felt as the fire crept closer.

In my mid-teens we stumbled across the place that became our last and best family holiday destination, a stretch of coast near the harbour of Solva in Pembrokeshire, a few miles from St David's. Some more friends (my parents were always richer in friends than in money) owned a small caravan at a campsite called Nine Wells, near to the sea, and for five or six summers we stayed in that tiny caravan, the four of us squeezed up together even as my sister and I grew into adults.

It must have been difficult for my parents, but it was the only way we could afford a two-week holiday at peak time, so we all made do. My father told me years later that he had been suffering from particularly bad depression during that time, and that the cramped caravan had aggravated things to the point that he found himself looking one day at the cliffs and had to suppress the urge to jump. He said that it had ruined that area for him for a long time; he is only now learning to love it again, and the memories remain.

I had no idea. I thought it was idyllic. We were half a mile from the sea, and each day we would pack up our sandwiches and march down through a small wood out into a lush valley, where heather grew on the cliffs and wild ponies grazed. The trail sloped down towards the sea until at last we emerged onto the coast path, and made our way painfully down the rocks to an almost-hidden beach.

All at once we noticed the ominous flickering light, and peered around the back of the house to see that the mountainside above us was ablaze

This inlet is called Porth-y-Rhaw, and is almost non-existent when the tide is high. At low tide we sat for hours on hot rocks, padding down to swim occasionally in the water, which grew deep quickly. Despite being surrounded by cliffs, it was perfect for swimming, and my mother often swam right out around a huge rocky outcrop, a little arm waving from the glistening surface of the sea.

As I write this, my father has sent me a video he has just taken on his smartphone of my mother plunging into the water in that same cove. Sometimes returning is about being brave. In her seventies she leaps into icy seawater, emerging blue and shivering, and my father returns once again to the place where he had such vivid suicidal thoughts, sending us cheery photos and updates. They still go on holiday to Pembrokeshire most years. He still struggles with depression, particularly in the winter. These days it's rare that my sister or I can join them, although last year I went for a few days with my partner. He went fishing with my father, while my mother and I swam, and then walked to meet them. New memories start to overlay the old.

When I went abroad after university, on hot nights in Asia and Australia I thought longingly of the cool Welsh coast, splashing into deliciously cold water, and the sight of that beloved landscape, bleak and lush and wet and beautiful. As Arthur Ransome recognised, those places are indelibly part of me, wherever I am in the world and however many years pass. I'm missing a visit there this year, but I'll be back.

Returning to a childhood haunt as an adult must always be bittersweet, for we know that the summers, once endless, are now numbered, and one day the things and people that draw us there will no longer exist. We find new places, new habits, and eventually the vivid image of those childhood holidays fades into memory like the photographs we took, to be occasionally lifted down from the shelf and examined wistfully, before the present calls us away. H

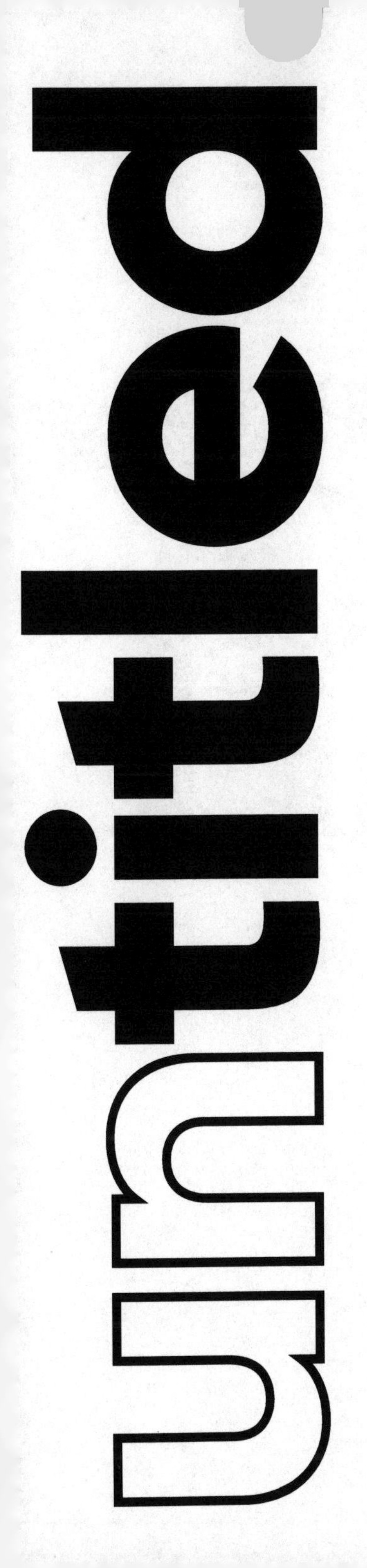
untitled

The Red Scarf

by Jennifer Y. Montgomery

When I was a child, my mother had a red, silk Japanese-print scarf. The eighties were a time of scarves and my mother had a vast collection. This one was broad and a dashing red too tomato to be crimson. It was crossed with beams of creamy white and had a giant teal circle rising up the center like an alien moon. I think the circle was what made me consider the scarf Japanese. It reminded me of the Japanese flag in the 'F' volume of the Encyclopedia Britannica. It was my favorite of her things.

Sometimes, after school, I would race home before my brother and sister. I would slip into my mother's room and pull the scarf from the central drawer of her dresser. I would unfold it and drape it over my head like a habit, breathing in the scent of my mother's soap. Other times I placed it over my shoulders like a cape, or I laid the scarf over my palms, facing upward, as if I were a lady-in-waiting presenting to a queen. Then I would carefully refold the scarf into a perfect square and put it back in its place. I never spoke of the scarf to anyone, for fear that mentioning how much I loved it would make my mother want to squirrel it away, to keep it back. Her possessions were often like grave objects. Ceremonial. And she withheld these precious things easily under the guise that, as children, we would surely break or lose them. In reality, I cherished this scarf with a reverence generally reserved for my favorite stuffed animals. I treated it as if it were sacred. It was. I would never have harmed it.

When my brother was about to graduate from high school, my mother asked him what he wanted for a graduation present. He didn't want money or a car like the other kids in his class. He wanted to drive from our home in North Dakota to California to meet my biological grandfather for the first time. My father was a police officer who was killed while on duty when my sister and I were almost three and my brother was five. Shortly after his death, my mother had piled us and all of our things into her dusty orange Ford Pinto. We drove to rural North Dakota where she had spent childhood summers on her aunt and uncle's farm. We left a tiny two-bedroom apartment with cacti on the hill for a creaky white farmhouse, endless fields, trees good for climbing, and vast gardens ringed with electric fences to keep out the deer. My mother remarried quickly. We lived a new life in our small farming town while my mother tried desperately to forget her past. Part of that forgetting meant holding us at a distance. It wasn't like that at first. Now, I sometimes cling to the memories of the early days before we started elementary school. Our mother gathered her children around her like a barn cat with kittens. I recall sitting in her lap in the afternoons while she sipped coffee and smoked horrible, tiny, menthol cigarettes. I loved inhaling the smell of coffee from her breath. It still feels like home when I smell coffee. As we got older, she became more and more distant. I would spend hours unsupervised under the lilac bushes that rimmed our yard. Or high up in the Octopus Tree, which we named for the five trunks that connected at its base. My brother may have had it worse, because he looked just like my biological father with the same face and dark blue eyes. My sister and I favored my mother in looks. Sometimes, it was a lonely childhood.

My mother was the talk of the town for a while. Beautiful widow from out-of-state, rail thin with auburn hair and face dotted with freckles. My new grandparents were hesitant to accept this California beauty queen with three small children. It was my stepfather's first serious relationship. He was only 25. She was 27. They met in June, were engaged by July, and married by November. Everyone speculated that my mother just wanted my stepdad for his stable job. It was far from the truth; she really did love him. More, I suspect, than she had ever loved our biological father. She found an acceptance in him. A safe place. My biological father had never been safe.

By the date of my brother's graduation, our house was a blue, two-bedroom ranch in an aging suburban neighborhood. We had moved from our small country town of Carrington to the city of Fargo so that my stepdad could go back to school after he had been laid off from his job working at a grain elevator. After he finished his degree in Agriculture, he stayed on at the university.

> **My mother was the talk of the town for a while. Beautiful widow from out-of-state ... My new grandparents were hesitant to accept this California beauty queen with three small children**

The basement of our new house was partially finished and had a large den with a bar. My parents fashioned two bedrooms on one side of the den out of wood paneling. My room at least had a door, albeit cheap and hollow. My brother's room had only a sickly peach and brown linen curtain that my mother made on her sewing machine. The outside walls of our rooms were painted cement, mine pale pink and my brother's a creamy white. My sister initially shared my room but had gotten her own by staging a protest when we were twelve; she threatened to run away from home. Her twin-sized bed was moved into the small piano room upstairs where it shared the tiny space with our giant, antique, upright grand. There was just enough room to turn around – barely. My sister had to place her dresser inside the closet and her turtle tank at the end of her bed. As a result, I got a massive bedroom in the basement to myself.

We had three telephones. One was in the kitchen, hanging on the wall by the back door. One was in my parents' room. And one was in the basement on the wall between my brother's room and mine. After I met my first boyfriend, I used to stretch the phone into my room at one in the morning. The cord was so short, I could barely reach it around the corner and under the door. I had to sit just behind the door crack and lean my head flat against the wall to talk.

My right arm swung out and my hand hit the sharp end of our wooden bannister ... I immediately knew that something was very wrong

On the morning of my brother's graduation, my mother was feverishly cleaning every surface in our house. Hers was the kind of OCD that required glass-topped coffee tables and pure white bathrooms so that she could see they were clean. She used to vacuum the living room carpet in one direction and then in the opposite direction so that the carpet didn't have any lines. The graduation ceremony was at eleven and we had a huge family party planned for one, with assorted sandwiches on small white cocktail rolls, cans of black olives, homemade pickles, potato salad, and chocolate cake with brown sugar frosting. My grandparents and several aunts and uncles were making the three-hour trek from their tiny rural places into the city.

The phone rang while my mother was vacuuming upstairs. I instinctively ran down the basement steps to grab the other phone, in case it was my grandma or an aunt asking for directions to the ceremony. As I cast down the steps, my right arm swung out and my hand hit the sharp end of our wooden bannister just between my pointer finger and second finger. I immediately knew that something was very wrong. The pain was deafening. It took over every ounce of me. I tried to stop but could do nothing to lessen my forward momentum. I skidded down to the base of the stairs and crumbled into a curl, holding my hand under me like a baby bird. My brother later told me that my scream had been more animal than human. He ran out of his room, lifted me up, and carried me to the couch in the den. My hand had immediately started to swell and blacken.

My brother ran to get my mother. I heard the vacuum turn off. She came down the stairs with some ice in a dish towel. I looked up at her and said quietly, 'I think my hand is broken. I need to go to the hospital.' She asked me to hold my hand up and wiggle my fingers. I lifted my hand; it felt leaden, like a weight held under water. I closed my eyes with the pain, and then reopened them. Again, she asked me to wiggle my fingers. I complied and watched my fingertips able to move what looked like a millimeter. She said brightly, 'You'll be OK.' She told me to come upstairs, then turned and walked away.

I followed her slowly, my hand resting in the ice. She went down the back hallway into her room. I sat gently on the end of her bed and watched her open her scarf drawer and take out her red scarf. 'This should be big enough. Isn't it pretty?' She made a triangle out of the red silk, looping it and tying it around my neck. Then, she gently placed my hand in the cradle of the fabric. By this time my hand was swollen to about double its normal size. My fingers looked foreign, like they belonged to someone else. The pain had deadened to a constant hum. I looked from my hand to my mother and back to my hand. I tried again quietly, 'I think I need to go to the hospital.' My mother said in her most chipper voice, 'We don't have time before Kenny's graduation. Let's see how it is when we get back.'

That was the end of it. I knew it the moment she mentioned the graduation ceremony. I was not going to the hospital. I was not going to get an X-ray or a cast. Slowly I stood up and left her room, went into the bathroom, and opened the medicine cabinet. I took four ibuprofen with a swig of tap water. My mother walked past the bathroom door and into the living room. 'She's fine,' she exclaimed hurriedly to the empty interior.

And I was. I sat silently through my brother's graduation ceremony; my hand held gently by the scarf. I laughed with my cousins. I took my cake into the backyard and watched tiny red ants crawling on the pink peony blossoms. That night, my sleep was a fever dream, hot and gnarled.

We left for California at four in the morning. I lasted about an hour before the pain became unbearable. I fell asleep with my head against the window and my swollen hand held against the van wall. I awoke to fierce throbbing. My stepdad stopped at a gas station and filled a cheap, plastic hotel ice bin with ice. I submerged my hand, eyes filling from the shock of it and wedged the bin between my outer thigh and the van wall. The upper rim of the ice bin began to cut a harsh line into the skin of my thigh. We stopped every hundred miles or so to refill the bin with fresh ice.

I knew it the moment she mentioned the graduation ceremony. I was not going to the hospital. I was not going to get an X-ray or a cast

On long car trips, we always drove straight through. No hotels or restaurants. We would stop only for gas and at any historical monuments along the interstate. My mother always called them 'hysterical monuments' and then laughed at her own joke. I vividly recall each stop of this trip, because it meant un-submerging my hand from its tomb, laying it in the now water-stained scarf, and trying to slowly get out of the van without making too much of an impact on the pavement. I didn't dare complain. Mostly because it wouldn't change anything, but also because I didn't want to steal my brother's plain excitement at travelling into the unknown of our past lives in California. So, I steeled myself and posed at every pioneer village and scenic overlook on the way. And gently smiled. H

Friends For

A Day

by Laura Steiner

Despite my unwillingness to do it, I ran the heartbreak marathon. Some days I ran quickly but most of the time I ran very slow.

Within the first 1000 metres, I broke into water. And when I became water, I met some ordinary people who turned out to be extraordinary characters that stood by the sidelines while I ran.

I met them randomly. Serendipitously. On the street. In the train. Inside their homes.

Other than the encounters I've written about here, I never saw these people again and I never got a chance to thank them. This is my way of saying thank you because my heart cracked and I never expected a complete stranger in a queue in London to stop the flood from drowning me.

Jones

Much like Jones. The guy I met in a queue to get into a bar in London, which sounds terribly English – the queue and the rain because it was, of course, raining that Friday night.

The bar was packed and the guy at the door was adamant; 'Nobody is coming in right now!' Luckily there was a smaller bar at the end of the road, with a tin roof outside. We all took cover. Jones carrying a viola case and myself holding a rollie in one hand and a tequila shot in the other.

'You play?' asked my friend with the fiery red hair when she came outside holding two more tequila shots and pointing to the case. Stockhausen was mentioned. I didn't know Stockhausen and, to be fair, I was too focused on the massive downpour because this terribly English story is not as terribly English as you might think; the rain was not London's usual faint drip but a cracking thunderstorm.

I grew up disliking the rain and craving the sunshine. I grew up in Bogotá where the Andes and the high altitude conspire to create a city that, for half the year, is covered in rain water.

Thunder scared me growing up. 'You'll be hit by lightning' was a turn of phrase used by my mother to keep me indoors when it rained, but then someone I knew got electrocuted in the kiddie park, and from then on grey skies over the Andes meant panic.

When I moved away from home thunderstorms became a lifeline back to Bogotá. That night was the first time in the four years since I had moved to London that I could recall a storm of tropical proportions.

Lightning brightened the tin roof above our heads and Jones held tightly onto his viola. He told us that he played as a solo musician. He was also part of a band whose name I don't recall but it was of 'the Stockhausen vibes' (I made a mental note to research the German musician) and 'when he needs a full set of strings on stage, with the DJ Bonobo.'

I am sorry, Jones, I didn't mean to spill tequila on your shoe when you mentioned that, but I really love Bonobo. There's heartbreak and there's Migration. Every single song on that album.

The relationship that had ended the week before was a long-distance one and migration was a touchy subject at best. Or non-migration, to be precise. I was in London and he was somewhere else, far away from London; we were both migrating our separate ways rather than towards one another.

'What do you do?' Jones asked, drying the tequila from his shoe.

'I write.'

'You what?' He raised his voice over the thunder.

I mimed myself holding a pen and writing mid-air.

'Can I read something?' he asked. Just then the thunder stopped and, without the need to yell over the storm, an awkward silence emerged between us. I tore a piece of paper from my notebook, scribbled down my website name – with a real pen – and said goodbye to Jones and his viola, who were skipping the other party.

The following Thursday the name Jones showed up in my inbox saying that he was playing

```
tonight with Bonobo at Alexandra Palace.
It turns out I have a spare ticket. You're
welcome to it if you fancy.
```

He told me he'd leave the ticket at the box office under someone else's name.

> **The heartbreak that night was inevitable. I recorded an excessive amount of videos that were meant for the one person I couldn't talk to**

YES. Yes, of course. Yes, definitely. Yes, thank you so much.

I went to the concert by myself. I managed to spot Jones on stage, but other than him I couldn't see any other familiar faces. Bonobo was excellent but the heartbreak that night was inevitable. I recorded an excessive amount of videos that were meant for the one person I couldn't talk to. Watching them was a bitter reminder that we were not going to share things between each other anymore.

By the time I left Alexandra Palace it was raining. I hoped that the serendipitous encounter with Jones that led to Bonobo was a sign that, much like the night under the tin roof, the water would eventually stop.

I never saw Jones or his viola again. But I did listen incessantly to Bonobo for the next four months.

My Neighbour

It was raining.

Again.

Another torrential downpour because when you're feeling like shit, the weather copies your insides. Or your insides copy the weather. In any case, there's poetry in sadness and poetry in rain, and sometimes the two coincide. The storm was not of tropical intensity, but it was strong enough to turn me into a wet dog. Wet, blonde hair. Wet, swollen eyes. Red like the packet of Marlboros I had just spotted someone on my block holding.

In the months that followed the breakup, my sadness had blended with smoking. I had been an on-off social smoker forever but when the breakup happened, the social aspect of it vanished. I wanted a rollie at all times.

When you're feeling like shit, the weather copies your insides ... There's poetry in sadness and poetry in the rain, and sometimes the two coincide

Rollies became my loyal companions.

I was sad and anxious, and smoking kept me company. Walking home that day, sorrow struck when Spotify failed to take my feelings into consideration and played a song by The National. I had finally learned that fighting the jab of sadness was pointless. I had to make space for it because missing didn't take privacy into consideration and the crying that resulted didn't care whether I was standing in the rain, on the tube, or waiting in line for a coffee.

I was a few steps away from home but didn't make it inside my building because I had to light a cigarette right now, and right now I was lucky enough to have been gifted a smoke by the owner of the pack of Marlboros, a guy with terribly crooked teeth. I preferred rollies but in times like these, cigarettes would do too.

I stood outside my building smoking and called a friend to go over the script I knew by heart. 'I said, he said, we said, could have, should have, didn't say, hoped to say.' I went around in circles like this for months. I tried so hard to know what had gone wrong, hoping that if I did, I could find a way to fix it. And if I could fix it, I wouldn't need to stand outside smoking a soggy cigarette.

'You must be freezing.' She had long hair, a perfect smile and a soothing voice.

'Sorry, I didn't mean to interrupt your call,' she whispered. 'I'll just wait here.' I'd never seen her before but it turned out that this woman who was waiting for me to finish my phone call before inviting me inside her house for tea, lived in the building next door to mine.

'Mint tea?' she asked. 'I'll make you a whole pot of it.'

'Or chamomile. Rooibos tea?' She offered Earl Grey too. I kindly refused her offer to sit in what I imagine was a perfectly lit living room. I was too cold and too wet to sit on someone's couch. Maybe I was nervous that if I went in, I would never leave her flat. Maybe I didn't want to give an explanation of why I was standing outside my building dripping wet. Mostly I just wanted to go upstairs and light another cigarette.

The People On Broadway Market That Day

It had been a couple of months since the start of the marathon but I seemed to have misplaced the map and I kept running back to the starting line. An elephant still sat on my chest every morning and I needed some direction. I sent X Love an email. I was after a sign of life. Had X Love died?

His social media presence pointed otherwise. But the sadness felt like someone had actually passed away and I wanted to get hold of the ghost. What I got instead was further evidence of what had been our fractured relationship.

Me: This is my version of what happened.
X Love: And this is my version.
Me: This is mine.
X Love: Well, look at mine.

It was very hot outside and my brain melted with confusion between his version and mine. What was true? And why did it matter anymore?

X Love was very much alive but the relationship was very much over.

I read his response walking down Broadway Market, my favourite street in London and the headquarters to my life in the city. It was only a matter of time before water would be shed on home turf.

I walked towards one of the canal locks, tethered my computer to my phone and re-read his email a number of times nearing insanity. The scene must have looked ridiculous: my backpack with all its contents – a computer, a notebook, *Notes On a Nervous Planet* by Matt Haig, four red pens, one blue one, a set of keys and a golden bike helmet – splattered on the floor and a girl crying and talking over the phone in Spanglish.

'Sí, yo sé. But I still don't get it,' I told my friend.

The first stranger to approach the Spanglish griever was a brave kid. 'Is everything OK?' he asked.

'Yes, thank you for asking,' I answered.

He turned around and waved his arms to his dad who was standing in the corner. 'She's fine dad! Just crying!'

I read his response walking down Broadway Market, my favourite street in London ... it was only a matter of time before water would be shed on home turf

Then there was the woman who got off her bicycle and asked if I needed anything. She could go get me water. Or a tissue? Maybe a chair? I declined and told her thank you, I'll be fine.

'Nah, you're gonna be great,' she yelled as she got on her bike again and rode off.

After her came an older guy carrying a boombox on his right shoulder, who signalled for me to get up from the floor and gave me a hug with his free arm. He nodded goodbye and went his way mumbling to 'This Must Be The Place' by the Talking Heads.

How did he know that was my favourite song?

Daniels

By all meteorological accounts that summer was uncharacteristically hot for England. So hot I even managed to get a tan under the London sun. Sadness turned my memories of that summer into thunderous rain, but that's not entirely true given the 30+ Celsius degree weather and the sunsets that lit up the Thames.

Life was mostly spent outdoors: at picnics, pubs, swims, picnics again, a day trip here and a day trip there, an endless reel of attempted distractions. By the end of summer, my bank account was looking less than impressive and I needed an extra, temporary job that would carry me through the fall.

My friend was exhibiting at the Design Biennale at Somerset House and she hired me to be the gatekeeper for her installation, *Silent Room*, an insulated wooden structure that aimed to give visitors a respite from the city's noise. I was hired to be the doorwoman, the person in charge of asking everyone to please remove their shoes when they walked up the stairs. Thank you very much – despite all the eye rolls I got that week.

Apparently it's not only tears that are best kept private. Most people really hate taking their shoes off in public.

Is it because they find it embarrassing to reveal their socks? Did we accidentally get too close when I asked you to remove your shoes? Are you offended?

But not Daniels.

Daniels had no problem showing his brown socks in public. So instead of having to convince him to take off his shoes, we sat on a bench by the entrance and caught up on what felt like a lifetime of stories while he waited for his turn to go upstairs.

There was the night he shared a stage with Michael Kane in a pub in South London singing a jazzy tune. We couldn't figure out the name of the song, but apparently the night had been warm. People drank pints and whiskey and cheered from their tables. The crowd went wild when Daniels finished his song.

There was his trip to Colombia in the '90s. 'Way before it was even cool,' he said.

'Or safe.' (Touché Daniels, my friend.)

And of his obsession with London. 'Hardly a better city,' he declared.

I was silent but the twitch in my face probably spoke for itself.

The love-hate relationship I'd always had with the city had turned really sour by the end of that summer. It was impossible not to feel like London held the entirety of my heartbreak in its streets.

I spent months blaming London for reflecting its own greyness onto my feelings. Mare Street had started to look bleaker than it usually did, the Central Line more crowded, the men far less attractive and the city even more existentially lonely.

In the past I had cherished its big city feel and enjoyed my anonymity, but if I was ever going to get close to the finish line, I needed the opposite. I needed community. People. Connection. A feeling of belonging.

I'd always felt like a small fish in a big pond in London, but when fall came around, I felt as if I was a tiny tropical fish swimming in a very big, very British ocean. And I was swimming against the current.

That day in Somerset House, I found rest on an island in the shape of a charming Londoner who was carrying a *London By Foot* city guide in an attempt to see his 'hometown with a different pair of eyes.' But I think Daniels knew London like the palm of his hand and that it was going to require more than a travel book to take him somewhere he didn't know. During the marathon, my eyesight had turned blurry so that everything appeared a sulky grey, but that afternoon there was not one cloud in the sky and I promise promise promise that on my way home I found an empty seat on the Central Line.

Anne

It was a Saturday morning and I was on my way to catch a train at Hackney Central when I saw her slumped up against the door of a cellphone shop on Mare Street. She was conscious but the words coming out of her mouth were incoherent.

'Are you OK?' I asked, to which she replied, 'I'm fine,' because what else was she supposed to say to a stranger?

Fine.

I've just fallen on the ground, but I'm fine. Badly hurt, *so fine.* Tears out in public, *really, I'm absolutely fine.*

But of course Anne wasn't fine.

Strangers started crowding around her. There was the drunk woman who was smoking two cigarettes at the same time, inhaling from one while the other one dangled from her lips. She kept telling Anne to just relax between inhales. There was the curly-haired woman who called an ambulance. The two Italian men who turned out to be nurses on their day off.

'Let's keep her still,' one of them instructed us.

'I like how you speak,' our patient mumbled with a smile.

And the man with dreadlocks who preached with a full Caribbean swag, 'You're gonna be OK sister!' and knelt on the floor to be closer to Anne.

When I asked Anne whether we could call a family member or someone close to her who could meet her at the hospital, all I got was a 'not today.' Did she have any family? Was Anne going to be alone in the hospital?

She held my hand and locked eyes with me. 'You are all beautiful, but why are you doing this?' she asked with tears swelling in her eyes and then tears swelling in my eyes because my recently broken heart recognised Anne's very broken heart. And I had a feeling her fracture wasn't recent.

She told us that she had worked as a psychiatric nurse for 37 years at Homerton Hospital. And that she had a cat named Lola. What she didn't tell us was that she was lonely. But she didn't need to say it, we could all feel it.

Anne kept saying thank you and squeezing my hand. We all smiled. A lot. And tried to distract her with questions while we waited for the ambulance to arrive.

When Anne finally left, we all let go of the good face we were putting on for her. Everyone's smile dropped. The two Italians shook their heads. The woman with two cigarettes in her mouth managed to sigh. One by one we broke into water.

I never answered Anne's question, but we were all doing it because it mattered. It mattered that she knew that she wasn't actually alone.

I knew it mattered because the same thing had been mattering for me since the starting line.

The Guy On The Train

He was wearing black jeans and a striped shirt. There was a black beanie on his head and two dangling silver earrings in his right ear. A jawline that could make anyone go weak at the knees.

Thank god I was sitting down.

The main character was re-cast. Nobody held auditions but we had a James Dean with a beanie ... And a writer who realised inside the train that she was still very much alive

I was scribbling furiously but everything I wrote was completely meaningless. I was doing everything in my power to restrain myself from making eye contact because my eyes would give me away immediately. If not, my sweaty palms. Or my increased heart rate. I'm pretty sure the whole train could hear my pulse.

It had been months of feeling nothing. Not even a glimpse of attraction. The likelihood of ever being attracted to someone again had been subtracted from my life. Romance out the window. But Guy-On-The-Train, I wanted to sleep with you so badly. What would it feel like to wake up next to you?

Good? Bad? Awkward? Easy? Would we go for coffee? Would we do this again?

We never got there but at least there was the daydream of someone new in this narrative. The main character was re-cast. Nobody held auditions but we had a James Dean with a beanie, hooped earrings and a killer jawline getting off at some busy station. And a writer who realised inside the train that she was still very much alive.

Penny

A leak erupted in my room. Water dripped onto the floor for two straight days staining a wall brown and burning a lightbulb because water has a way of finding cracks and coming out wherever it pleases.

In the midst of falling water, mould crept over the bedroom wall and spread into my bathroom. I was afraid for my lungs, so I booked an Airbnb close by and that's how I ended up at Penny's front door that winter night.

I like going into other people's homes and imagining what life would be like if I lived there. What if my bed was another bed or my breakfast table was different and what if my home smelled like this, would I sleep on the first or second floor?

The life I stepped into that night was set in an old English house in Homerton where the walls were covered with Russian propaganda posters, the kitchen table had a bowl full of juicy oranges and a nearby cabinet was stocked with all kinds of teas.

This life also had a big grey dog. And the

memory of a cat who had passed away two days before. It was a house that was still in mourning.

The first night I stayed in Penny's house, she was adamant about showing me a photo of her late 16-year-old fluffy black cat. She scrolled for a long time on her phone to find a photo and she confessed with a hint of guilt that she had stopped photographing her cat when the dog arrived. 'But I loved that cat so much,' she explained.

I told her I had never had a pet, a fact about my childhood that I very much resented. Maybe if I'd had a dog growing up, things would be different now. Maybe not having a dog growing up is why I had such a hard time letting go of others. I never mourned a pet.

'That must be really hard,' I said, referring to her late cat.

We went silent for a while and then she said to no one in particular, 'the heart, you know?'

I did know.

Silence again.

'And your heart?' Straight to the point, Penny.

My heart was very confused. For months, I genuinely thought I was not going to survive the elephant that sat on my chest every morning, but then it was winter, the days were short and my bathroom was full of mould but somehow the elephant had turned into a lizard that was still heavy but was not going to kill me.

'Give it time,' people had said. People who I had wanted to punch because, if anything, heartbreak had stopped time. The seasons changed, my alarm went off every morning, and I turned 30, but for months time came to a standstill and every day felt the same.

But it turns out that even something as huge as love is subject to something as mundane (or is it grandiose?) as time. Time took a whole lot of time but it eventually did its thing. One day I realised I hadn't cried in a week. Sundays were all of a sudden a fine day. I was all of a sudden good company for myself again.

But where had the pain gone? Was it waiting for someone to play The National? Was it waiting to attack me in my dreams? On the dance floor? In the shower?

Time shrank the pain that kept me breaking into water in the most inconvenient places and moved it somewhere else, somewhere I didn't have to look at it constantly.

Heartbreak had kept X Love close – a little too close – and, even though it was painful, it had also kept my feelings alive. I hated losing someone but I hated even more losing love. Heartbreak had become a testament to that feeling and I was afraid of love itself going away.

As I said, when winter came around my heart was very confused.

'It's OKish,' I said to the woman who had recently lost her cat. But I don't think she was listening to me. She was already too busy feeding her new dog. H

Lessons on the Western Front

by Peter Pool

Bo is almost at the geographical centre of Sierra Leone in West Africa. When I lived there in the 1980s, it was a peaceful place. In Bo you were well insulated from the stress and clamour of the so-called developed world; there were no telephones and shortwave radio reception could be elusive. My copies of *The Guardian Weekly* usually turned up in clumps, a few weeks late. Day-to-day life in Bo had a clockwork predictability to it. With Sierra Leone being near the equator, sunrise and sunset changed little throughout the year and the weather felt repetitive: hot and humid every day, except during the rainy season when it was hot, wet and humid. The only real deviation from this was the Christmas Harmattan, a cool wind blowing in from the Sahara, which produced fog. This was a welcome relief for northern expatriates, but it sent Sierra Leoneans fetching their pullovers and lighting bonfires to keep warm.

The absence of electricity and running water was well factored into daily life, and no one found it worthwhile to talk about such things. Occasionally a senior politician would come to Bo for a weekend and bring oil for the town generator. Then my dusty electric light bulbs would suddenly sport a harsh glare, far too bright for eyes that had become used to the gentler yellow flames of candles and kerosene lamps. It was tempting to switch them off, whilst enjoying the comforting sound of a purring electric refrigerator.

Part of the clockwork movement of town life involved the faded orange bus that belonged to Bo Teachers' College. It made the journey each weekday morning from Bo town out to the college campus, four miles away at Towama, carrying the staff and students who did not live on campus. When I had an early class to teach, I would drive out from Bo and, a few minutes ahead of the bus, my Land Rover would quickly fill with the Sierra Leonean staff waiting at various points along the roadside. It took a little while for me to develop the eye needed to spot them and for them to work out how best to catch my attention, but it soon became a regular habit and was a congenial way to start the day. The process reversed at the end of the morning session as I sensed eyes watching for when I might be departing college. If I left at the very end of the morning, I took care to include the raucous market lady who ran a food stall on the campus. She would start shouting for me to wait while she got her pots and pans together, and then squeeze into the back of the vehicle with all her hardware, a little bit Widow Twankey style. As we made our way back into Bo town, more shouting and the banging of pans told me when she wanted to get out. It was a pantomime performed in high spirits with much amusement – very Sierra Leonean in the way that the simplest of transactions could produce a sense of being glad to be alive – and I found great joy in being part of it.

Two days each week I visited primary schools out in the villages, ten or twenty miles from Bo town, to give Maths workshops to teachers. These worked well provided I took enough rice for everyone to have a meal at the end. The drawback was that two-thirds of the way though the workshop, the female teachers would absent themselves to go and cook the food. I never found a way around this problem but a very tasty meal appeared, so a good time would be had by all… and perhaps this is what it was all about. Thoughts I might have had that I was passing on hard knowledge that would, in some modest way, help to create a better future were soon tempered by the discovery that years previously someone working in an earlier aid initiative had imparted information and ideas very similar to those I was offering… but little had changed. No, I was offering a brief boost to the morale of poorly paid teachers, who often felt neglected: that was my contribution.

Within a few minutes a bespattered teacher in not much more than a loincloth appeared with a plastering trowel in hand.

From time to time, I visited primary schools to see individual teachers. The essential requirement for this was that the school should know I was coming, otherwise I could easily end up disappointed by what I might find. I turned up in one village to find no shortage of children, but the school buildings deserted. As I got out of my vehicle, I surveyed the scene, and the scene surveyed me: a child suddenly shot off. Within a few minutes a bespattered teacher in not much more than a loincloth appeared with a plastering trowel in hand. Cheerfully, he explained that he was repairing one of the classroom walls and that the children were helping to farm. He offered me a chair in the shade whilst he sent a child to fetch the head teacher. A charming young man soon appeared, apologising for not knowing about my visit. The teacher I had come to see had, apparently, not passed on the message to the school and had himself gone off to a funeral – I kept a straight face at hearing this, it was a familiar story whenever someone wanted to avoid a meeting – but wouldn't I stay and have a drink of palm wine? The sun was getting high, and it was hard to refuse.

Soon, a boy came with a plastic gallon container of the milky white liquid. Palm wine, which is the fermented sap of palm trees, was deceptively easy to drink, provided you did not mind straining it through your teeth to remove the floating detritus in it. I did my best to avoid too many refills of my plastic beaker as the young head teacher started to explain some of his problems. They grew a lot of cassava in the village but he needed petrol to run his cassava grater. It was a twenty-mile walk to get some… and the cost was so great. I was all too conscious of my Land Rover dominating the scene. It rose almost as high as the school building and contained at least half a tank of petrol. We talked on, about how hard life was out in the bush and so, finally, I said that if he had a tube long enough, we could siphon some petrol out of my tank. This was soon effected and there was a good feeling all round as we had another drink of palm wine.

I set off back to Bo in high spirits along the rough, deserted track, with the hot breeze blowing over me, and soon picked up a good speed. Twenty minutes later the sudden appearance of the T-junction, where I needed to go left, brought me out of my daze. I slammed on the brakes and, to the awful grating sound of tyres on loose gravel, skidded across the road, coming to a halt just a few yards short of a mud brick house that, had I braked only seconds later, I could have quite easily demolished.

—

On school visits I often took a teacher supervisor with me from the Ministry of Education in Bo. On one occasion, I remember picking up the portly, and usually ebullient Mr Koroma, just as he was walking out of the marketplace. He was not in a good mood. After an uneasy silence and a sucking of teeth, he announced, 'I would rather live in South Africa than here. At least in South Africa they have enough to eat.'

'Mmm, yes, but in South –'

'I cannot afford to feed my family!' he continued. 'I need at least two bags of rice each month and I cannot afford even one. It is a disgrace for me. I don't mind being a second-class citizen if I can feed my children. Those black people in South Africa – they are better off than we are in Sierra Leone! I am ashamed.'

Rice came in 50kg bags and this was the usual currency by which people measured their salaries. It was the time of year when locally grown rice was not available, so it had to be imported, and prices were now at a previously unheard-of level. A few weeks after Mr Koroma's rage of shame, a lecturer at the college drew me aside. He seemed uneasy as he talked around and around without quite coming to the point. Finally he stuttered out that he needed some money to feed his family… could I lend him...? I didn't do loans, but I began to share his embarrassment and simply gave him some money.

I slammed on the brakes and, to the awful grating sound of tyres on loose gravel, skidded across the road, coming to a halt just a few yards short of a mud brick house

Afterwards I wondered if he would tell anyone, because then I would be getting more requests than I could cope with, and they would be hard to refuse. No one approached me, but I started seeing my surroundings in a different light. Another lecturer would periodically ask me about scholarships to study in Britain. He was quite open about it: life was becoming very difficult in Sierra Leone and Britain would be a better place. I asked what would happen with his wife and family, if he left. He would send money for them, he assured me, though he didn't sound that convincing. College lecturers were part of the narrow layer of the middle class in Sierra Leonean society. If they were finding it difficult, how was it for the vast numbers below them?

Later in the term, we had a rare college staff meeting to discuss timetable plans for the coming year. There were three expatriates left on the staff; we rarely said much about how the college ran, sensing that this was not our party, and in this particular case, two of us would not be there the following year. At the meeting it was suggested that classes could be doubled to reduce teaching demand. The idea that 60 students could be squeezed into classrooms designed for 30 appeared not to trouble anyone. I couldn't see how it could be done physically, never mind the quality of the teaching that would result; already the students were academically weak. I listened to this discussion, waiting for someone to say what seemed obvious to me. But no one raised any objections. Finally I spoke up, conscious of my privileged position, and said, as politely as I could, how incomprehensible it all seemed. I think my input helped quash the idea, though I felt sure it would return sooner or later. It might have been that the White Man's voice still carried some vestigial authority, deserved or otherwise. Or did they feel the need to preserve appearances in front of strangers?

the familiar BP logo became NP – National Petroleum – but it was not long before people would tell you sardonically, that NP stood for No Petrol

Afterwards I reflected on it all. I knew that some of the Sierra Leonean staff taught in local secondary schools as well as at the college and I had seen this as a willingness to help out with teacher shortages.

It meant that some classes at college were without their lecturers from time to time, not least because of the difficulty of getting transport from Bo town out to the college. Then it dawned on me that the altruism of lecturers teaching in schools and college at the same time might not be quite what it seemed. Had they simply discovered a way of earning two salaries when one was clearly not enough?

For the whole of my time in Sierra Leone, the economy was in decline. You could always be caught out by the next unexpected shortage: flour, tins of sardines, tomato paste. Onions were usually sold in the marketplace in piles of four or five, but I once saw individual onions being sold by the slice – cut up as though they were tiny melons. In my last year there, the exchange rate was declining rapidly and the cost of a humble ballpoint pen was getting to be out of reach, even for a teacher, whilst children struggled to hold stubs of pencil scarcely two or three centimetres long in their tiny fingers. Fuel shortages came and went, but Sierra Leoneans never lost their sense of humour. When the oil company BP finally pulled out and transferred its assets to the government, the familiar BP logo became NP – National Petroleum – but it was not long before people would tell you sardonically, that NP stood for No Petrol. H

/ **Aftershocks**

by Hannah Storm

An aftershock follows a larger earthquake, in the same vicinity as the main tremor. It can inflict its own damage and is caused as the crust that is displaced by the earthquake adjusts to the effects of the trauma.

Bougainvillea mask the smell of blood, before their petals fall to the ground. In the morning the hotel staff will have swept away any evidence the flowers were once here. Just their scent will remain. Beneath us the ocean will bloom a dazzling Caribbean blue and from up high Haiti will look like paradise.

The girls too, click-clacking onto the hotel terrace in their heels, will be gone. But on this night in December 2004, they are knock-kneed Bambis, swaying beneath the crystal strands of chandeliers that bump each other in the breeze, whispering of the women brought here by men who could be their fathers.

I catch her smile, the girl across from me, watch as she reapplies her petal pink lipstick and he tightens his hold around her waist. He kisses her with total disregard for what she's so lovingly applied: the makeup that means more to her than he will ever know. To him, it was an afterthought grabbed from the drug store where he stocked up on condoms because he knows he's not dumb.

She does not flinch when the soundtrack changes, when Simon and Garfunkel sticks in mid-song, when 'The Sound of Silence' is shattered by the pop-pop of gun fire rising on the thermals.

—

I remember the carrion I saw this morning, swooping above the parched river beds that have become graves in districts named after dreams not nightmares. Belair and Cite Soleil – *Beautiful Air* and *Sun City* – where night spells rest only for the dead, the stench of their bloated bodies rising in the hot sun.

Darkness brings danger to the living. Without electricity, a power cut means more than the absence of light. Here men creep from the shadows and savage young girls with their rifles and gang rape.

I hear their stories from the soldiers who are meant to protect them, from the peacekeepers who only come here by day, because even for them in their armoured vehicles the dark is too much.

Come morning, they drive their military personnel carriers on patrols through the potholed streets, their presence a pretence. Today I went with them, rattling through the damaged veins of Cite Soleil, beneath a low and unusually warm winter sun.

The sky above our heads was the same clear cobalt as the Caribbean, just metres away. Birds of prey soared and sank, their shrieks like the screams of those alive enough to fear death. The smell of those already silenced invaded my nostrils, clung to my skin, my clothes. The salty sea air could not blow it away.

Beneath palm trees, tiny children hunted through piles of rotting garbage, for treasures to fill their distended bellies. Dust spun from the tracks of the tank, painting their skin a ghostly grey. They turned their spectral faces towards us, smiling as if the soldiers were saviours on white stallions. We all waved.

Just then, a bullet split the air above our heads, forcing us into the belly of the metal beast. My borrowed bullet proof vest, far too big for my female frame, rode up like the shell of a tortoise, smashing my chin and the heavy helmet slipped and smacked my nose. When I emerged from beneath my body armour, the soldiers were staring at me. 'A virgin, boys', one of them said in Portuguese, and their laughter ricocheted around the vehicle's inside.

—

Now I nurse my drink, still in the sweat-soured shirt and pants that smell of death and disdain. My shoulders ache from the weight of my loaned flak jacket. My chin and the bridge of my nose are scraped and bruised. I empty my glass, noting how much easier each successive sip is after the first, which seared my throat.

Night has fallen. The sky is pierced with stars, but beneath us there is only black. I think of the girls mutilated by men with guns – children too young to have bled who now haemorrhage, raped by those who bear arms so violently that some of their victims will never bear children. The men force themselves into the girls, one after one, sowing their seeds inside their tiny bodies. Those who give birth to the children of their rapists don't know the names of the men who stole their pasts and futures.

And yet, the United Nations and the authorities are helpless against the militias who maraud through the neighbourhoods by night. Here in Haiti in 2004, rape is a weapon in a war that the world largely ignores.

She said she wished they had riddled her body with bullets instead and how, for nine months, she prayed for death

I remember the girl I met yesterday, rocking her baby in her arms, shushing it with the same lullaby she must have learned on her mother's knee little more than a decade earlier. Her words were whispers and as she sang, a tear traced a line down her cheek seeking out the contours of a scar by her lip.

She said she had not seen their faces in the dark. But she smelt them, heard and felt them. She said she wished they had riddled her body with bullets instead and how, for nine months, she prayed for death. Now she clung to the tiny life in her arms, knowing she would do anything possible to protect her daughter.

Years later, I think about the two of them as I nurse my own daughter.

I remember how the young woman sat in the shady garden of the refuge where she had been given a home, beneath the flowers blooming pink and purple. I remember thinking how very young she looked. Her features have faded in my memory, but I picture her reaching to wipe away a tear, her fingers feathering the scar. The men split her face with the butt of the rifle when she screamed, silencing her, scarring her. I remember how she leant into her sleeping baby, kissing her unblemished face. I remember the look of love she gave her infant daughter whose name I don't recall but somehow, I think she was called Luce, which means 'Light'.

—

The first of my own sexual assaults took place in August 2004. I was in the Dominican Republic, the country that shares the island of Hispaniola with Haiti, because Brazil, the World Cup Football Champions, were staying the night there. The next day I would fly with them as one of a small group of journalists invited to report on a match against the national side: a friendly game designed to promote peace in Haiti.

Trauma memories are not like normal ones. They are fractured and unformed. Years of trying to piece together the jigsaw pieces ... and there are still gaps

As the only female reporter, I knew I would be seen as both a novelty and a liability. Little did I know I would be too much of both and one of the men connected to the team would take advantage of my place in the order and disorder of things by assaulting me.

I say one of them because I still do not know who it was.

Trauma memories are not like normal ones. They are fractured and unformed. Years of trying to piece together the jigsaw pieces of that night, and there are still gaps.

This is what I remember.

I stepped out of the elevator onto the wrong floor, to the fizz of a failing hotel generator, the close heat of a Caribbean summer, the headiness of anticipation, the warmth of an evening's conversation with colleagues fuelled by alcohol.

Before I even registered my mistake, the stranger's hands were tearing at my green dress. For years I persuaded myself that in dressing in the same colour as the footballers, it made me somehow complicit in this assault. Recently I found an online clip of the game, and realised they had not worn green, and I was not to blame. Back there in the dark corridor, this man yanked the crossovers of my bodice like he was ripping open an envelope. In the dark, I could not make out his features, but I could taste him and smell him.

I still cannot remember how it physically ended. I think I fled down the hotel fire escape. I know I sought out someone I trusted, someone who I saw as a friend and colleague – a man connected with the team who had been instrumental to me being invited on this trip. He convinced me to stay quiet about what had just happened.

So I did. For 14 years.

I did not know on this sultry summer evening on the edge of the Caribbean that this sexual assault would compel me to persuade my news organisation to let me return to Haiti a few months later as a freelance journalist.

I did not know that in order to do so I would have to agree to go on a journalism safety course where I would meet a man who would go on to abuse me for many years. I did not know that I would become pregnant by this man the following year. I did not know this would happen just a few weeks after visiting the Brazilian man whom I had trusted and told about my initial assault, who had instead told me to stay quiet. I did not know that this initial betrayal would be followed by a more bitter one when he would invite me as a friend to his city, warn me of its dangers and then rape me while another man watched us.

I did not know that, despite these horrors, I would become a single mother to my own ray of light. Or that when my daughter was three I would return to Haiti after a massive earthquake shattered the country, killing unknown numbers of people. Or that when I did, I would convince my boss to send me to cover the disaster because I was the only person in the newsroom who knew Haiti. I did not yet know these things and I did not yet know myself.

—

My first visit to Haiti was supposed to be a celebration – a day when the world's most famous footballers did their bit for global peace, cementing their hero status in one of the world's poorest countries. And I had the privilege of being invited along as the only foreign female reporter. No matter that the game, originally touted as a 'peace match', where Haitians would give up their guns for a ticket, had become something of publicity stunt by the Brazilian president Lula, whose country was leading the United Nations mission to keep peace in a country wracked by conflict and corruption. No matter that the stadium would be packed with the wealthy and well-connected. No matter that I would fail to produce anything of quality because I would spend the whole ninety minutes of the game seeking out the person who had assaulted me. No matter that journalists are supposed to be able to recognise famous footballers. No matter that heroes can be abusers too.

[The] doors opening to an oven of heat ... the roar of a crowd competing with the engines of the plane

That day we landed in a Brazilian plane, its doors opening to an oven of heat the likes of which I had never experienced, the roar of a crowd competing with the engines of the plane. From there it was into armoured personnel carriers driven by Brazilian soldiers, part of the same peacekeeping mission I would encounter during my later visit to Port-au-Prince. In front of us a gleaming white stallion of a vehicle paraded through the streets, carrying the famous footballers who held the World Cup high in the air, a glistening trophy. They waved like conquering heroes returning from battle.

The green flags of Brazil fluttered in the slight breeze, their motto 'Ordem e Progreso'.

Still, nobody here seemed to be bothered by their

false promise of peace, order and progress. Today these men brought hope to a country beleaguered by recent unrest, bloodshed and killings. Today, the road from the airport to the stadium was thronged with people.

They stood in stagnant water, clung to trees, balanced on corrugated iron roofs of breezeblock and wooden homes, teetered on top of abandoned vehicles. Many wore the colours of their heroes, others modelled t-shirts printed with the faces of the footballers. The noise was so loud that, when I tried to record my voice into the mini-disc, I couldn't hear myself speak.

I see their faces in the haunted bodies of the young girls orphaned by the earthquake, who have lost their mothers, who cry out to me for water

Men, women and children cheered their names. 'Ronaldo, Ronaldinho, Roberto Carlos,' they chanted, and with every name I felt the shape of his mouth over mine, the tug of his fingers on my flesh and wondered, was it him?

—

Back in the hotel bar in Haiti four months later, I am the only foreign female. The young woman across from me turns and offers a thin smile. It's different from the one she gives the man who brought her here and for a second the lights that drip from the ceiling outline her lips and I think I see a scar's tell-tale shine there too. I touch my fingers to my face, feeling for the words we might share if we could speak across this space owned by men, wonder what silences she keeps as her means of survival.

My next visit to Haiti will not come for another five years, and only after an earthquake has torn the fabric from beneath the feet of this country's people and this hotel has collapsed into the dust, taking with it the secrets of its past.

But the memories will not fade. Not of those who tottered through the bar walking as if on unstable ground. Or those whose scars show and those whose scars don't. I see their faces in the haunted bodies of the young girls orphaned by the earthquake, who have lost their mothers, who cry out to me for water, who I want to sweep into my arms and hold until the shaking stops and the pain subsides. And long after I leave, I will think of them and the countless others whose secrets have been buried in the collapse of this country. H